Shades of Dawn

Biography

By Nadia Sinclair

Copyright © 2024

All rights reserved.

ISBN: 979-8-9915679-3-0

Copyright Page

Shades of Dawn
Copyright © 2024 by Nadia Sinclair – Pen name
All rights reserved.

No part of this book may be reproduced, distributed, or transmitted in any form or by any means, including photocopying, recording, or other electronic or mechanical methods, without the prior written permission of the publisher, except in the case of brief quotations embodied in critical reviews and certain other noncommercial uses permitted by copyright law. For permission requests, write to the publisher at the address below:

Nadia Sinclair
Orlando, FL
USA
This is a work based on a true story. Names, characters, places, and incidents have been changed to protect the privacy of individuals. Any resemblance to actual persons, living or dead, or actual events, is purely coincidental.

ISBN: 979-8-9915679-3-0

Dedication

This book is a personal journey, written by myself but made possible with the unwavering support of dear friends who stood by me every step of the way. Your encouragement, belief, and strength have meant the world, and for that, I am forever grateful.

To those who seek beauty and courage in every moment, even when the world seems dark and unyielding. Your determination to find light in the shadows is a testament to the resilience of the human spirit.

For Jasmine—whose strength, grace, and quiet resilience have been a constant source of inspiration. You have shown us all that even in the harshest of seasons, one can bloom. May your story serve as a reminder that true courage comes from within, and that even in the face of overwhelming challenges, inner beauty and strength will always shine through.

This is for all the dreamers and fighters, for those who refuse to give up, and for those who understand that the most beautiful stories often arise from the deepest struggles.

Acknowledgment

This novel would not have been possible without the unwavering support and encouragement of many incredible individuals.

First and foremost, I want to thank my family for their endless love and patience throughout this journey. To my friends, your belief in me provided the motivation to keep going, even when the path seemed uncertain.

To my readers, thank you for embarking on this journey with Jasmine. Your enthusiasm and feedback have been a constant source of inspiration.

Lastly, to Jasmine, the heart of this story—may your resilience and grace inspire all who read your tale. Thank you for reminding us that beauty and strength can flourish even in the most unexpected places.

Table of Content

Copyright Page *2*
Dedication *3*
Acknowledgment *4*
About the Author *7*
Chapter 1 .... *9*
  Roots and Beginnings 9
Chapter 2 .... *27*
  Whispers and Shadows 27
Chapter 3 .... *42*
  Dreams of Escape 42
Chapter 4 .... *57*
  Building a New Life 57
Chapter 5 .... *71*
  Seeking Truths and New Beginnings 71
Chapter 6 .... *83*
  Stability and Healing 83
Chapter 7 .... *101*
  Blossoming Love and New Beginnings 101
Chapter 8 .... *114*

    Navigating the Challenges 114

Chapter 9 132
    Unraveling Trust and Betrayal.................................. 132

Chapter 10 146
    A New Awakening.. 146

Chapter 11 155
    A Mother's Despair 155

Chapter 12 172
    A Life of Questions and Despair 172

Chapter 13 188
    Embracing a Solitary Path 189

Conclusion.. 201
    A Journey of Resilience and Hope 201

Other Works by N. Sinclair............................... 206
    Author's Page:... 206

About the Author

Nadia Sinclair is a versatile writer who effortlessly navigates through various genres, including contemporary fiction, third-party biographies, drama, personal development, self-help, and more. Her ability to weave compelling narratives across diverse themes has earned her a dedicated readership and critical acclaim.

Nadia's creative journey is fueled by her love for life's simple pleasures. She often finds inspiration during serene moments at the beach, where the rhythmic waves provide a perfect backdrop for her thoughts. Whether sipping on a steaming cup of coffee or a calming tea, Nadia immerses herself in stories, both written and read, drawing endless inspiration from the world around her.

Her passion for storytelling is matched by her commitment to personal growth, both in her characters and her readers. Nadia believes that through the power of words, we can explore the depths of human experience, uncovering truths that resonate and inspire.

With each book, Nadia Sinclair invites readers to embark on a journey of discovery, promising a blend of heart, wisdom, and unforgettable tales. Whether delving into the complexities of human relationships or guiding readers toward self-improvement, her writing is a testament to her belief in the transformative power of stories.

Chapter 1

Roots and Beginnings

A Vibrant Town

Jasmine's story begins in a small, bustling town in North Africa. The town was a vibrant tapestry of sights, sounds, and smells, where the rhythm of life was dictated by the call to prayer and the hum of activity in the souks. Narrow, winding streets were lined with whitewashed buildings, their wooden shutters painted in vivid blues and greens. The air was often filled with the fragrant aromas of spices, freshly baked bread, and the occasional waft of incense from the local mosques.

In the heart of the town, the souk was a bustling marketplace where merchants hawked their wares under colorful awnings. Stalls overflowed with a dazzling array of goods: vibrant fabrics, intricate silver jewelry, handwoven carpets, and fragrant spices piled high in pyramids. The shouts of vendors bargaining with customers mixed with the clamor of people, the braying of donkeys, and the laughter of children playing in the narrow alleys. This was the world where Jasmine was born and raised, a place where tradition and community thrived amidst the chaos.

Family and Early Years

Born into a modest family, Jasmine's early years were marked by the absence of her parents' presence and a series of profound changes. Her parents, Nora and Jamal, had separated when she was just a baby, leaving her to be raised by her grandmother, Salma. Though her mother lived only a few blocks away, and her father in a distant city, neither played a significant role in her upbringing.

Salma was a nurse at the local hospital, a position she had worked tirelessly to achieve after starting as a janitor. Her journey from cleaning floors to treating patients was a testament to her resilience and dedication. Each promotion came with its own set of challenges and learning curves. Salma often stayed late at the hospital, pouring over medical books and manuals, determined to master every aspect of her job. Her colleagues admired her tenacity and often sought her advice on difficult cases. Salma's hands, though rough from years of hard work, were gentle and skilled, bringing comfort to countless patients.

Jasmine's Admiration

One evening, Jasmine sat beside Salma as she tended to their small garden. The scent of blooming jasmine flowers mingled with the earthy aroma of freshly turned soil.

"Grandmother, how did you become a nurse?" Jasmine asked, her eyes wide with admiration.

Salma smiled, her hands pausing in their work. "It wasn't easy, Jasmine. I started as a janitor, cleaning floors and emptying trash. But I was determined to learn and grow. With time and effort, I worked my way up."

Growing up under Salma's care, Jasmine was acutely aware of the sacrifices her grandmother made. Salma's stories of her late husband who died in the war, and her journey from a janitor to a nurse were the bedtime tales that shaped Jasmine's understanding of perseverance and dedication. Jasmine admired her grandmother deeply, drawing inspiration from her strength and determination.

The Hospital as a Second Home

The hospital itself was a bustling hub of activity, much like the souks of the town. The corridors echoed with the sounds of patients and staff, and the sterile smell of antiseptics was ever-present. Jasmine often accompanied her grandmother to the hospital, where she spent many afternoons in the small staff room, doing her homework and reading books while Salma attended to her duties. The nurses and doctors became familiar faces, often stopping by to chat with Jasmine and share stories of their own.

"You're becoming a regular here, Jasmine," one of the nurses, Fatima, would say with a smile. "Maybe you'll join us one day."

These experiences instilled in Jasmine a deep respect for the medical profession and a desire to one day make a difference in the world. Jasmine would nod eagerly. "I want to be a nurse like Grandmother."

Simple Life

Life with Salma was simple but filled with love and lessons. Despite the struggles, Salma ensured that Jasmine's needs were met, both materially and emotionally. She made sure Jasmine attended school, emphasizing the importance of education as a means to a better life.

On weekends, they would walk through the souk, the bustling marketplace that was the heart of the town. Stalls overflowed with vibrant fabrics, intricate silver jewelry, handwoven carpets, and fragrant spices piled high in pyramids.

The shouts of vendors bargaining with customers mixed with the clamor of people, the braying of donkeys, and the laughter of children playing in the narrow alleys. One day, as they passed a stall selling books, Jasmine's eyes lit up.

"Can we buy one, Grandmother?" she asked eagerly.

Salma smiled, her eyes twinkling with affection.

"Of course, my dear. Education is the key to a better life."

Nora's Absence and Bitterness

Jasmine's mother, Nora, was a less constant figure in her life. Living only a few blocks away, she had remarried and started a new family. Visits from Nora were infrequent and often tense.

Nora harbored bitterness towards Jasmine's father, Jamal, which she did not hide from her daughter.

"He's a bad man," Nora would say, her voice filled with contempt. "You don't need to know anything about him or his family."

This narrative was echoed by Salma, who also warned Jasmine against any contact with her father's side of the family. Despite the fear instilled by her family's warnings, Jasmine's curiosity about her father grew as she did.

Unanswered Questions

The secrecy and hostility surrounding any mention of him only heightened her desire to uncover the truth. She wondered what he was like, what kind of family he had, and why he had never tried to contact her.

Why was her father "so bad?" What had he done to make her mother and grandmother despise him so much?

These questions swirled in her mind and the mystery of her father's absence formed a shadow that loomed over her otherwise bright childhood.

"Grandmother, why does Mother hate Father so much?" Jasmine asked one afternoon as they tended to their small garden.

Salma's hands, usually so steady, paused in their work. She looked at Jasmine with a mix of sadness and resolve.

"Your mother and I have our reasons, Jasmine. It's best that you don't concern yourself with him. Focus on your future, not the past."

Her voice was gentle but firm, leaving no room for further questions. Jasmine nodded, sensing the finality in her grandmother's tone, but the unanswered questions continued to haunt her.

As she grew older, Jasmine began to piece together bits of information from overheard conversations and occasional slips by her mother and grandmother. She learned that Jamal had also remarried and had other children. This knowledge added another layer of complexity to her feelings. Why did her father care for his other children but not for her? The sense of abandonment was a wound that never fully healed.

Jasmine vowed that one day, she would find the answers she sought.

Books as an Escape

Salma, aware of Jasmine's growing curiosity, tried to divert her attention by involving her in various activities. She encouraged Jasmine to focus on her studies and pursue her interests. Jasmine excelled in school, her grandmother's encouragement fueling her ambition. She became a voracious reader, finding solace and adventure in books. The characters she read about became her friends, their stories a temporary escape from her own.

Books transported Jasmine to different worlds, allowing her to explore places and lives far removed from her own. She devoured novels about strong, independent women who overcame great odds, finding in them reflections of her grandmother's resilience. Her love for reading also fostered a curiosity about the world beyond her small town. She dreamed of traveling, seeing the places she had read about, and experiencing new cultures and adventures.

Friendships and Community

Jasmine's friendships also played a crucial role in her development. Her best friend, Maria, was a constant companion, sharing Jasmine's adventures and dreams. Maria's family owned a small café near the souk, and many afternoons were spent there, sipping sweet mint tea and sharing stories. Maria's parents were kind and welcoming, often treating Jasmine like another daughter.

One evening, as the sun set over the town, casting a golden glow over the rooftops, Jasmine and Maria sat on the steps of the café, watching the world go by. The air was filled with the sounds of evening prayer, a soothing backdrop to their conversation.

"Do you ever wonder about your father?" Maria asked, her voice gentle. She knew of Jasmine's curiosity and the pain it caused her.

"All the time," Jasmine admitted. "I just want to know why he never tried to contact me. Why does he seem to care for his other children but not for me?"

Maria nodded; her eyes filled with sympathy. "Maybe one day you'll find out. And maybe it won't be as bad as you think."

Pursuing Dreams

For now, Jasmine channeled her energy into her studies and helping her grandmother. Salma's tireless work at the hospital and the life lessons she imparted to Jasmine became the foundation upon which Jasmine built her dreams. She envisioned a future where she could rise above the challenges of her past and create a life filled with purpose and fulfillment.

Despite the shadows of her father's absence and the secrets surrounding her family, Jasmine's spirit remained unbroken. She held onto the values her grandmother had instilled in her: hard work, determination, and the belief that she could overcome any obstacle. As she stood on the threshold of adolescence, Jasmine's journey of self-discovery and the quest for truth was just beginning.

Life in the North African town continued to shape Jasmine in countless ways. The vibrant community, with its mix of tradition and modernity, was a constant source of fascination and learning. The town's festivals, with their colorful processions and lively music, were occasions that

Jasmine looked forward to every year. She loved the sense of unity and joy that these celebrations brought, a reminder of the strength and resilience of her people.

A Garden of Memories

One summer afternoon, as Jasmine helped her grandmother tend to their small garden, she mustered the courage to ask again about her father. The garden was a sanctuary for both, a place where they could escape the hustle and bustle of daily life. The scent of blooming flowers was creating a peaceful atmosphere.

"Grandmother, why does Mother hate Father so much?" Jasmine asked, her voice barely above a whisper. She watched as Salma's hands, normally so steady, paused in their work.

Salma sighed deeply and wiped her hands on her apron, looking at Jasmine with a mix of sadness and resolve. "Jasmine, your father... made choices that hurt us deeply. It's not something I can explain easily."

"But why doesn't he ever try to contact me? Doesn't he care about me at all?" Jasmine's eyes filled with tears, her voice trembling with a mix of anger and sorrow.

Salma reached out, gently brushing Jasmine's cheek. "It's complicated, my dear. Sometimes adults make mistakes, and those mistakes have consequences. Your father... he has his own life now, with a new family."

Jasmine nodded, wiping away her tears with the back of her hand. "I just want to understand. I feel like there's a part of my life that's missing."

Salma hugged her tightly, whispering in her ear, "I know, sweetheart. I know. But you have me, and you have a future ahead of you. Focus on that. One day, maybe you'll find the answers you're looking for."

As Jasmine stood in the garden, surrounded by the comforting presence of her grandmother and the familiar scents of home, she felt a small sense of closure. She didn't have all the answers, but she had the strength and determination to keep searching for them. And in that moment, she realized that her journey of self-discovery was just beginning.

Chapter 2

Whispers and Shadows

Curiosity and Confusion

As Jasmine grew into a teenager, her curiosity about her father's absence and her mother's animosity only intensified. Her childhood had been marked by a lack of answers, and now, as she stood on the cusp of adulthood, the need for truth burned within her like an ember. She had learned to navigate the bustling streets of her North African town with confidence, but the mysteries of her own life remained an uncharted territory that she longed to explore.

Whenever Jasmine broached the topic of her father, Nora's response was always the same: a sarcastic look followed by a stony silence. This routine left Jasmine feeling both confused and alone, her questions met with a wall of disdain. Despite the fear that her father's "ugly and scary" image had instilled in her, her curiosity about him and the reasons behind her mother's hatred continued to grow.

Secret Conversations

Nora and Salma often sat close together; their heads bent in hushed conversation. They whispered so that Jasmine would not hear, but she could sense that they were discussing matters of great importance. These secretive talks only fueled her suspicions. What were they hiding? Why was she forbidden from knowing anything about her father?

One evening, after another frustrating encounter with her mother, Jasmine decided she could no longer remain silent. She confronted Nora directly, her voice trembling with a mix of anger and desperation. "Why don't you treat me like your other kids? Why do you hate me?"

Nora's eyes narrowed, and she gave Jasmine a sarcastic look before turning away. "You wouldn't understand," she muttered, her voice cold and dismissive.

Jasmine felt a pang of hurt and frustration. "But I want to understand! I deserve to know why you're like this."

Nora's silence was the only answer Jasmine received. The lack of explanation left her feeling more isolated than ever, her questions hanging in the air like unresolved chords.

A Bond Tested by Manipulation

Salma and Jasmine shared a special bond, one built on mutual love and respect. They often spent afternoons together, caring for their little garden, the fragrance of jasmine flowers blended with the earthy scent of freshly tilled soil. They laughed and shared stories, their companionship providing Jasmine with a sense of stability and warmth.

This peaceful relationship, however, was frequently disrupted by the manipulative influence of Nora. Each time She visited Salma's demeanor shifted dramatically. The woman who had been so gentle and nurturing would suddenly become cold and critical. Jasmine noticed the change immediately: the warmth in Salma's eyes dimmed, replaced by a stern, disapproving glare.

Nora's whispered words seemed to transform Salma, turning her against Jasmine for reasons she couldn't understand. The pain of these moments was profound, as Jasmine felt the sting of betrayal not just from her mother, but from her beloved grandmother as well. Despite the manipulation, Jasmine clung to the cherished moments with Salma, hoping that the bond they shared could withstand Nora's divisive tactics.

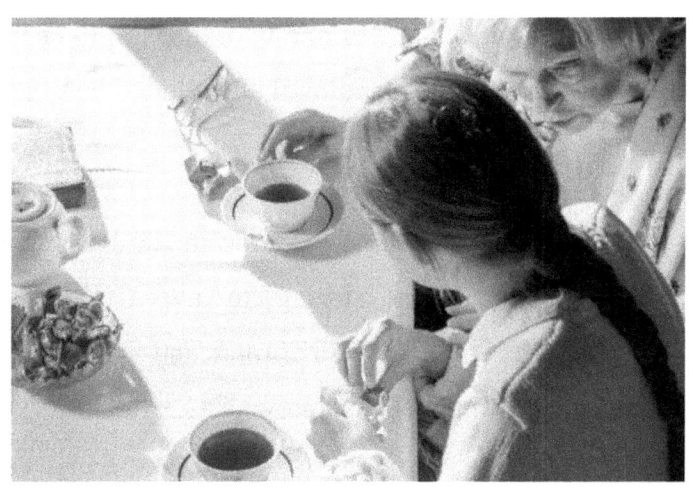

Growing Hostility

As a teenager, Jasmine was trying to make sense of her life and her situation. She had countless questions but no Answers. The whispers between Nora and Salma grew more frequent and intense, and Jasmine couldn't shake the feeling that she was at the center of their discussions. The more she tried to eavesdrop or piece together snippets of conversation, the more elusive the truth became. The hatred between Nora and Jasmine escalated as Jasmine grew older. Nora continued to create problems between Jasmine and Salma, exploiting her influence over the older woman to make Jasmine's life increasingly difficult. Every night, after work, Nora would come over, sit next to Salma, and whisper in her ear. They would glance at Jasmine with disdain, their looks filled with a shared understanding that excluded her.

Hiding in the Basement

Jasmine spent most of her time in the basement of her grandmother's house, trying to avoid Nora. The basement, with its cool, dimly lit corners and the faint smell of damp earth, became her sanctuary.

She spread her textbooks out in front of her, immersing herself in her studies to escape the tension that filled the house whenever Nora was around.

Jasmine could hear the faint sound of Nora's voice upstairs, already filling the house with tension. She took a deep breath, bracing herself for the inevitable confrontation once Nora left.

Jasmine's phone buzzed, and she saw a message from her friend Maria: "How are you holding up?"

"Surviving," Jasmine typed back. "Trying to stay out of sight."

Manipulation and Abuse

After these visits, Salma's behavior towards Jasmine would change. The slightest mistake, a floor not mopped to perfection, clothes not folded neatly would set her off. She would yell at Jasmine, her frustration spilling over into anger. Jasmine knew that Nora was manipulating Salma, turning her against her granddaughter. The realization that her own mother was the source of her grandmother's sudden outbursts left Jasmine feeling betrayed and bewildered.

Nora seemed to enjoy getting Jasmine into trouble with Salma. It was as if she derived some twisted satisfaction from seeing Jasmine punished and humiliated. Jasmine could not understand why her mother harbored such resentment towards her. She wondered if it had something to do with her father, but without any concrete answers, she was left to speculate in the dark.

Salma was kind to Jasmine when Nora was not around, but the moment Nora appeared, Salma would transform, often withholding even basic necessities like food at Nora's insistence.

Jasmine endured extreme hardship during this time. For almost an entire year, Jasmine survived on nothing but bread and tea, her meals a reflection of the hardships she faced, while Nora took Salma to her house and cooked delicious meals for her. The contrast was stark and cruel, deepening Jasmine's resolve to leave.

One day, her friend Maria brought her yogurt. As Jasmine savored each spoonful, she marveled at its creamy texture and subtle sweetness, feeling as if it was the most delicious food she had ever tasted. This small act of kindness from Maria provided not just physical nourishment, but a glimmer of hope and a reminder of the simple joys that still existed in her life.

Despite the constant tension, Jasmine continued to excel in her studies, knowing that education was her ticket out of this toxic environment.

An Overheard Revelation

One night, as Jasmine lay in bed, she overheard her mother and grandmother talking in the next room. Their voices were low, but Jasmine could make out enough to understand that they were discussing her aunt Nayla, Jamal's sister. Her heart raced as she strained to hear more, but the conversation abruptly ended, leaving her with more questions than answers.

The mention of Nayla intrigued Jasmine. She had never met her aunt and knew very little about her, but she felt a sudden urge to find her. Determined to uncover the truth about her family's secrets, Jasmine decided she needed to meet Nayla. She waited for the right moment, and one afternoon, when Nora and Salma were both preoccupied, she sneaked out of the house.

A Secret Meeting

Navigating the dark streets of her town, Jasmine felt a mix of excitement and fear. She had managed to gather some clues about Nayla's whereabouts from overheard conversations and the few times she had dared to ask about her. After a long walk, she finally found herself standing in front of a modest house on the outskirts of town.

Taking a deep breath, Jasmine knocked on the door. Moments later, a woman who looked strikingly like her father opened it. Nayla's eyes widened in surprise when she saw Jasmine. "Jasmine?" she asked, her voice filled with a mix of disbelief and warmth.

"Aunt Nayla?" Jasmine replied tentatively.

Nayla pulled her into a tight hug, her embrace warm and affectionate. "I can't believe you're here," she said, her voice trembling with emotion. "I've missed you so much."

Finding Comfort

Jasmine felt a wave of relief wash over her. She had finally found someone who seemed genuinely happy to see her. Nayla invited her inside, and they spent hours talking. Although Nayla was tight-lipped about the details of the family feud, she offered Jasmine comfort and reassurance. "Hang in there, Jasmine," she advised. "Focus on building your future. Things will get better."

Nayla's words were a balm to Jasmine's wounded heart. She began to visit her aunt in secret, finding solace in their clandestine meetings. Nayla's house became a refuge where Jasmine could escape the hostility at home and feel truly cared for. Each visit strengthened their bond and provided Jasmine with a sense of belonging that she desperately needed.

Seeking Answers

During these visits, Jasmine often complained about Nora's behavior towards her. Nayla listened patiently, offering her support and understanding. "Your mother has her reasons," Nayla would say gently. "But that doesn't excuse the way she treats you. Just remember, you're strong and capable. Don't let anyone make you feel otherwise."

Nayla's encouragement helped Jasmine cope with the challenges at home. Despite the continued hostility from Nora and the manipulation from Salma, Jasmine found a renewed sense of purpose. She threw herself into her studies, determined to build a future that would allow her to escape the confines of her troubled family life.

Graduation Day

Jasmine stood proudly in her cap and gown, holding her diploma. She had done it—she had graduated high school. Despite all the obstacles, she had achieved her goal. Salma smiled at her, pride evident in her eyes. "I'm so proud of you, Jasmine," she said, handing her a small velvet box. "This is for you."

Jasmine opened the box to find a beautiful necklace. "Thank you, Grandmother," she said, tears of gratitude welling in her eyes.

Nora, who had been standing nearby, scowled. "She doesn't deserve that," she snapped, grabbing the box from Jasmine's hands. "You're wasting your money on her."

Salma's face fell, and she reluctantly took the necklace back. Jasmine's heart broke a little more, but she didn't let it show. She had more important things to focus on—like getting out of this toxic environment.

The Seeds of Rebellion

One evening, as Jasmine prepared to leave Nayla's house, her aunt handed her a small, wrapped package. "This is for you," Nayla said with a smile. "Open it when you get home."

Curious, Jasmine took the package and thanked her aunt. Later that night, in the privacy of her room, she unwrapped it to find a beautiful, intricately designed journal. Inside the front cover, Nayla had written a note: "For Jasmine, to record her dreams, thoughts, and everything in between. Never stop believing in yourself. Love, Aunt Nayla."

Jasmine felt tears well up in her eyes as she read the note. The journal became her confidant, a place where she could pour out her heart and make sense of her feelings. It was a small but significant gesture that reminded her she was not alone.

Enduring the Storms

As the years went by, Jasmine continued to visit Nayla in secret, drawing strength from their bond. Her aunt's unwavering support gave her the courage to face the difficulties at home and the resolve to pursue her dreams. The shadows of her family's secrets still loomed large, but Jasmine knew she had the inner strength to navigate the darkness and find her own path.

Despite the challenges, Jasmine's spirit remained unbroken. She held onto the values her grandmother had instilled in her: hard work, determination, and the belief that she could overcome any obstacle. With Nayla's love and encouragement, Jasmine began to envision a future where she could rise above the pain of her past and create a life filled with purpose and fulfillment.

Chapter 3

Dreams of Escape

Academic Excellence and Ambitions

Jasmine continued to excel in her academics, her focus sharper than ever. She dreamed of immigrating far away to the United States to pursue a career that would allow her to help others, just as her grandmother Salma had done. The allure of a new beginning in a place where she could escape her mother's toxic grip was a powerful motivator. She spent countless hours studying, her mind fixed on the future.

"One day, I'll get out of here," Jasmine would often tell herself, flipping through pages of her textbooks late into the night. The basement, her sanctuary, became a place of intense learning and quiet determination.

The Search for Opportunities

Hoping to find a way to escape, Jasmine looked for opportunities to study or work abroad. She applied to universities and scholarship programs in multiple countries, each application a step closer to her dream. Her dedication to her studies paid off, earning her top grades and the admiration of her teachers.

"You're one of the brightest students I've ever taught," her science teacher, Mr. Amin, told her one day. "With your grades and determination, you can go far."

"Thank you, Mr. Amin," Jasmine replied, her eyes shining with hope. "I'm doing everything I can to make that happen."

The Breakthrough

Jasmine's hard work paid off when she earned her college degree and received an acceptance letter from a school in the United States. The process of obtaining a visa was arduous, requiring a mountain of paperwork and numerous visits to the embassy. But Jasmine persevered, driven by the vision of a new life far away from Nora's control.

One afternoon, as she sat in the basement, surrounded by piles of documents, her phone buzzed. It was an email notification. With trembling hands, she opened it and saw the words she had been praying for: "Your visa application has been approved."

Reactions at Home

The day Jasmine received her visa was the happiest day of her life. She rushed upstairs to share the news with Salma, her heart pounding with excitement.

"Grandmother, I got it! I got the visa!" Jasmine exclaimed, her voice filled with joy.

Salma looked up from her knitting, her eyes wide with surprise and pride. "Oh, Jasmine, I'm so proud of you! You've worked so hard for this."

Salma's emotions were mixed. She was genuinely happy that Jasmine would have the opportunity to build a bright future, yet a deep sadness lingered as she realized how much she would miss her granddaughter. Salma's eyes shone with pride and tears, capturing the bittersweet moment perfectly.

Jasmine hugged her grandmother tightly, feeling a mixture of relief and anticipation. "I can't believe it's finally happening. I'm going to America!"

However, Nora's reaction was starkly different. When Jasmine informed her mother of the news, Nora's face hardened, her eyes narrowing with anger.

"You're not going anywhere," Nora snapped. "You belong here with your family. Who's going to take care of your grandmother?"

"Grandmother can manage without me," Jasmine replied, her voice steady. "I've earned this opportunity, and I'm taking it."

Nora's opposition and desire to keep Jasmine under control became even more evident. "You're just running away. Do you think life will be better there? You're making a big mistake."

Jasmine felt a pang of guilt but knew she had to leave. "I have to do this for myself, Mother. I need to get away and build a future."

The Final Farewell

The weeks leading up to Jasmine's departure were a whirlwind of preparations and emotions. Salma helped her pack, offering words of wisdom and encouragement.

"Remember, Jasmine, you're strong and capable. Don't let anyone make you feel otherwise," Salma said, her voice filled with warmth.

"I won't, Grandmother. Thank you for everything," Jasmine replied, her eyes glistening with tears.

On the day of her departure, Jasmine stood at the doorway, her suitcase beside her. The reality of leaving her home, her grandmother, and even her tumultuous relationship with Nora hit her hard. She felt a knot of mixed emotions—fear of the unknown, excitement for a new beginning, and sadness for the life she was leaving behind.

Nora stood with her arms crossed, a scowl on her face. "Don't think you can come running back when things get tough," she said coldly.

Jasmine took a deep breath, trying to steady her nerves. "I won't. I need to do this."

Salma stepped forward, hugging Jasmine tightly. "Take care, my dear. And write to me often."

"I will, Grandmother. I promise," Jasmine whispered, holding back her tears.

The Flight to the USA

As Jasmine boarded the plane, she felt a wave of fear and excitement wash over her. The enormity of what she was about to do settled in. She was leaving everything she knew for a new world, one filled with possibilities and uncertainties.

Sitting in her seat, she looked out the window as the plane took off, the town she had known all her life shrinking below her. She felt a pang of sadness but also a surge of exhilaration. She was finally free.

During the long flight, Jasmine's mind raced with thoughts of the future. What would life be like in the United States? Would she be able to succeed in her studies? Would she find the peace and happiness she longed for?

Arriving in a New World

When the plane landed, Jasmine felt a mixture of relief and anxiety. The bustling airport, with its endless stream of people and signs in English, was overwhelming. She clutched her suitcase tightly, navigating her way through customs and immigration.

"Welcome to the United States," the immigration officer said with a smile, stamping her passport.

Jasmine smiled back, feeling a sense of accomplishment. She was here. She had made it.

As she stepped outside the airport, the unfamiliar sights and sounds of her new environment hit her. Tall buildings, busy streets, and a sea of people from different backgrounds—it was a stark contrast to her small town in North Africa.

Mixed Feelings and New Beginnings

Jasmine felt a mix of emotions—fear of the unknown, excitement for the future, and a lingering sadness for the life she had left behind. She took a deep breath, reminding herself of the reasons she had come here. She was determined to build a new life, pursue her dreams, and make her grandmother proud.

She found a taxi and gave the driver the address of the student housing where she would be staying. As the taxi wove through the city streets, Jasmine's eyes were wide with wonder. The city was alive with energy, a constant buzz of activity that was both intimidating and exhilarating.

When she arrived at the student housing, Jasmine felt a surge of nervousness. She checked in and was shown to her small, sparsely furnished room. It wasn't much, but it was hers—a place where she could start anew.

Settling In

Over the next few days, Jasmine worked on settling into her new life. She familiarized herself with the campus, attended orientation sessions, and met other international students who were also adjusting to their new surroundings.

One evening, she sat at her desk, writing a letter to Salma. "Dear Grandmother, I made it safely to the United States. The city is so big and different from home, but I'm excited to be here. I miss you already, but I know this is the right decision. I'm determined to make you proud."

As she sealed the envelope, Jasmine felt a sense of connection to her grandmother, even though they were now oceans apart. She knew that Salma's strength and wisdom would always be with her.

Facing Challenges

Despite her excitement, Jasmine quickly realized that adapting to life in a new country was not without its challenges. The cultural differences, the academic rigor, and the distance from her family weighed heavily on her. There were moments of doubt and homesickness, times when she questioned whether she had made the right decision.

One evening, feeling particularly overwhelmed, Jasmine called Nayla. "Aunt Nayla, I miss home. Everything here is so different, and sometimes I feel so alone."

Nayla's voice was reassuring. "It's natural to feel that way, Jasmine. You've taken a big step, and it's not going to be easy. But remember why you left and what you're working towards. You have the strength to get through this."

Jasmine took comfort in her aunt's words. "Thank you, Aunt Nayla. I'll keep pushing forward."

New Friendships and Opportunities

As time went on, Jasmine began to find her footing. She made friends with fellow students, joined study groups, and immersed herself in her studies. Her determination to succeed fueled her, and she began to see the fruits of her hard work.

One day, as she walked through the bustling campus, she realized how far she had come. She had navigated countless obstacles, faced her fears, and was now building a life that was truly her own.

Jasmine's journey was just beginning, but she was ready to face whatever challenges lay ahead. She had the support of her grandmother and aunt, the memories of her past, and the strength she had gained from her experiences. With each step forward, she was forging a path toward a future filled with hope and possibilities.

A New Dawn

Standing on the balcony of her student housing, Jasmine watched the sunrise over the city. The sky was painted with hues of pink and gold, a symbol of new beginnings. She felt a sense of peace and determination. This was her chance to create the life she had always dreamed of.

As the sun rose higher, Jasmine whispered to herself, "I can do this. I will make a difference. And I will make Grandmother proud."

Chapter 4

Building a New Life

A New Beginning

Jasmine's transition to life in the United States was filled with excitement, challenges, and the promise of a better future. She threw herself into her studies, determined to excel and make the most of the opportunities before her. The bustling city and the diversity of people and cultures were a stark contrast to her small North African town, and Jasmine found herself both overwhelmed and invigorated by her new environment.

One evening, as she walked through the campus, taking in the sights and sounds of her new world, she felt a sense of accomplishment and hope. She was forging her own path, free from Nora's control and the shadows of her past.

Meeting Sam

It was during her second year of college that Jasmine met Sam. He was charming, attentive, and seemed genuinely interested in her and her dreams. They met at a student event, and from their first conversation, Jasmine felt a connection.

"Hi, I'm Sam," he said, extending his hand with a warm smile.

"Jasmine," she replied, shaking his hand and feeling a spark of excitement.

Their relationship blossomed quickly. Sam was supportive and encouraging, and Jasmine felt safe and cherished in his presence. They spent hours talking about their hopes and dreams, and for the first time in a long while, Jasmine felt truly happy.

Marrying Sam

Within a few months, Jasmine and Sam decided to get married. It was a small, intimate ceremony attended by a few close friends. Jasmine's heart swelled with joy as she looked into Sam's eyes and said her vows.

"I promise to love and support you, no matter what," Sam whispered, his voice filled with sincerity.

"And I promise to stand by you, through all the ups and downs," Jasmine replied, her eyes glistening with tears of happiness.

The Arrival of Amal

Shortly after their marriage, Jasmine discovered she was pregnant. The news filled her with a sense of wonder and anticipation. She was going to be a mother, and she was determined to be the best mom she could be.

When their daughter, Amal, was born, Jasmine felt a surge of love and protectiveness. Holding Amal in her arms, she made a silent vow to always be there for her, to give her the love and support that Jasmine had longed for in her own childhood.

"She's beautiful," Sam said, looking at their newborn daughter with pride.

"Yes, she is," Jasmine replied, her heart full.

With that, she turned and walked back inside, ready to embrace the challenges and opportunities that awaited her. Jasmine's journey of self-discovery and the quest for a better life had only just begun, and she was more determined than ever to succeed.

Sam Showing His True Colors

The joy of motherhood was soon overshadowed by Sam's changing behavior. As the months passed, Sam's true colors began to emerge. He became increasingly irritable, controlling, and demanding. The man who had once been so supportive and loving was now someone Jasmine barely recognized.

"Why is the house always such a mess?" Sam snapped one evening, his voice harsh and accusatory.

Jasmine, exhausted from taking care of Amal and trying to manage the household, tried to calm him down. "I'm doing my best, Sam. It's not easy with a baby."

"Your best isn't good enough," he retorted, his eyes cold and unfeeling.

The Birth of Elias

A year after Amal's birth, Jasmine discovered she was pregnant again. This time, the news was met with mixed emotions. She was overjoyed at the prospect of welcoming another child, but she also feared how Sam's behavior might affect their growing family.

When their son, Elias, was born, Jasmine felt a renewed sense of hope. Holding her baby boy in her arms, she prayed that this new life would bring positive changes.

However, Sam's behavior only worsened. He continued to abuse Jasmine, both physically and emotionally, and used her like a maid, catering to his every need while he offered no help to the children. The dream of a loving family felt increasingly distant, replaced by a daily nightmare of fear and oppression.

Sam took advantage of Jasmine's vulnerability, knowing she had no family to turn to for support or protection. His abusive behavior grew unchecked, fueled by her isolation. Jasmine's lack of a support system made her an easy target, and Sam's cruelty left deep emotional scars, highlighting the devastating impact of isolation and abuse.

Enduring the Abuse

Jasmine was an educated and strong woman who had immigrated to the United States on her own, escaping a past filled with manipulation and control. Being put under a man's thumb, subjected to his abuse and dominance, was intolerable. Yet, she endured the suffering for the sake of her kids, hoping to shield them from the trauma of a broken home.

Jasmine tried to make it work, enduring Sam's brutality and manipulation.

During this period, Sam's behavior became increasingly erratic and controlling. He isolated Jasmine from friends and any support system she might have developed. He cut the phone lines to prevent her from calling the police and spread rumors that she was mentally unstable, discouraging others from helping her. The isolation was suffocating, and Jasmine felt more trapped than ever before.

Despite Sam's growing volatility, Jasmine hoped things would improve. She believed in the vows they had made and clung to the memories of the loving man she had married. Whenever Sam lashed out, he would eventually apologize, promising to change.

"I'm sorry, Jasmine," he would say, his voice filled with remorse. "I didn't mean to hurt you. I promise I'll do better."

Jasmine wanted to believe him. She wanted to believe that the man she had fallen in love with was still there, beneath the anger and harsh words.

Jasmine's Strength

Despite the abuse, Jasmine's strength became her greatest asset. She refused to let his behavior break her spirit. She focused on her children, pouring all her love and energy into caring for Amal and Elias.

One evening, as she sat in the nursery, rocking Elias to sleep, she whispered to herself, "I have to be strong for them. They need me."

Jasmine knew she had to find a way out. The turning point came when Sam's abuse escalated to physical violence. Jasmine knew she had to leave for the sake of her children. She reached out to her friend Leslie, who had always been a source of support and encouragement.

Planning to Leave

"Leslie, I need your help," Jasmine said, her voice trembling. "I can't stay here anymore. Sam's behavior is getting worse."

Leslie's response was immediate and resolute. "You and the kids can stay with me. We'll figure this out together."

With Leslie's help, Jasmine began to plan her escape. She gathered important documents, packed essentials, and waited for the right moment. One night, when Sam was out, Jasmine took Amal and Elias and fled to Leslie's house.

A New Beginning

Living with Leslie provided Jasmine with a sense of safety and relief. She focused on rebuilding her life, finding a job, and securing a place for herself and her children. The road ahead was challenging, but Jasmine was determined to create a better future for herself and her kids.

One afternoon, as she watched Amal and Elias play in the backyard, she felt a sense of peace and determination. "We're going to be okay," she whispered to herself.

The Custody Battle

Sam did not take Jasmine's departure lightly. He contested the custody of Amal and Elias, leading to a protracted and painful custody battle. Jasmine found herself in and out of court, fighting to protect her children from the man who had caused them so much pain.

During one particularly grueling court session, Sam's lawyer tried to paint Jasmine as an unfit mother. "Your Honor, Ms. Jasmine has no stable income and is living with a friend. This is not a suitable environment for the children."

Jasmine, though shaken, stood her ground. "Your Honor, I may be living with a friend, but my children are safe and loved. I have found a job, and I am working hard to provide for them. They need stability, and I am committed to giving them that."

The judge listened carefully, weighing both sides. After several agonizing weeks, the decision was made in Jasmine's favor. She was granted primary custody of Amal and Elias, with Sam receiving supervised visitation rights.

Reclaiming Her Life

With the custody battle behind her, Jasmine focused on reclaiming her life. She found a small apartment for her and her children, creating a safe and nurturing home environment. She worked tirelessly, balancing her job and her responsibilities as a mother.

One evening, as she tucked Amal and Elias into bed, she felt a sense of accomplishment and peace. "We did it," she whispered, kissing their foreheads. "We're going to be okay."

Jasmine's journey had been filled with challenges, but she had emerged stronger and more determined than ever. She had reclaimed her life and was building a future filled with hope and possibilities.

Moving Forward

As the years went by, Jasmine continued to grow and thrive. She built a support network of friends and colleagues who admired her resilience and strength. She watched with pride as Amal and Elias flourished in school, their laughter and joy a constant reminder of why she had fought so hard.

One day, as she sat on the porch, watching her children play, Leslie joined her, a cup of tea in hand. "You've come a long way, Jasmine," Leslie said, her voice filled with admiration. "I'm so proud of you."

"Thank you, Leslie," Jasmine replied, her eyes shining with gratitude. "I couldn't have done it without you."

Leslie smiled, placing a hand on Jasmine's shoulder. "You had the strength all along. You just needed a little help to see it."

As they sat together, sharing a moment of quiet reflection, Jasmine felt a deep sense of peace. She had faced immense challenges and had come out stronger on the other side. Her journey was far from over, but she was ready for whatever lay ahead, knowing that she had the strength and resilience to overcome any obstacle.

Jasmine's story was a testament to the power of hope, determination, and the unwavering strength of the human spirit. She had built a new life, filled with love and purpose, and was ready to face the future with courage and confidence.

Chapter 5
Seeking Truths and New Beginnings

The Lingering Curiosity

Despite building a new life for herself and her children, Jasmine's curiosity about her past remained. It no longer consumed her every thought, but the desire to uncover the truth about her parents lingered in the back of her mind. She often thought about the fragments of conversations she had overheard as a child and the secrets her mother and grandmother had kept from her.

One evening, after putting Amal and Elias to bed, Jasmine sat on the porch, sipping tea and staring at the stars. The night was calm, but her thoughts were restless. She picked up her phone and dialed her Aunt Nayla's number.

"Nayla, it's Jasmine," she said when her aunt answered. "I need to know the truth about my parents. I'm an adult now, and I think I deserve to understand what happened."

There was a pause on the other end of the line before Nayla responded. "Jasmine, you are right, you deserve to know the truth. I'll tell you everything."

The Conversation with Nayla

Jasmine settled into her chair, gripping the phone tightly. "Please, Aunt Nayla. I need to know why my mother and father split up and why everything was kept a secret from me."

Nayla took a deep breath and began. "Your mother, Nora, and your father, Jamal, had an arranged marriage. They were never truly happy together. Nora had an affair, and when Jamal found out, it shattered their already fragile relationship."

Jasmine listened intently, her heart pounding.

"Your father pressed charges and Nora ended up in jail for weeks for infidelity," Nayla continued. "Salma had to sell her house and her gold to bail her out. In our culture, it's a very bad thing for a woman to cheat on her husband. The shame and dishonor were unbearable for Jamal. He decided to leave and start a new life elsewhere."

"Why did Nora take her anger out on me?" Jasmine asked, her voice trembling.

"Every time she saw you, she saw Jamal," Nayla explained gently. "You were an innocent reminder of her mistakes and the life she lost. It's not fair, but that's the truth."

The decision to Reach Jamal - Her Father

Upon discovering the truth about her parents, Jasmine was stunned by the revelations and overwhelmed with a mix of shock and relief. Tears streamed down her face as she felt a surge of mixed emotions—anger and sadness at the years of deceit, but also a profound sense of connection and belonging she had never known.

"I need to talk to him, Aunt Nayla. I need to hear his side of the story."

Nayla hesitated. "Jamal is living in Canada now with his new family. I have his contact information. I'll give it to you."

Jasmine took a deep breath and wrote down the phone number Nayla dictated. She knew this was a crucial step in her journey of self-discovery.

Calling her Father

That evening, Jasmine sat at her kitchen table, staring at the phone. She took a deep breath and dialed the number. It rang several times before a voice answered.

"Hello?"

"Hi, is this Jamal?" Jasmine asked, her voice shaking.

"Yes, who is this?"

"It's Jasmine... your daughter."

There was a long pause. "Jasmine? I... I can't believe it."

"I need to see you, Father. I need to talk to you and understand why you left and never looked back."

Jamal sighed. "Alright, come to Canada. We can talk."

Planning the Trip

Jasmine began planning the trip with her kids, Amal and Elias. She explained the situation to them, trying to prepare them for the journey ahead.

"Mom, are you sure about this?" Amal asked, her eyes wide with concern.

"Yes, sweetheart. I need to do this for myself and for you both. It's important to understand our past," Jasmine replied, her voice filled with determination.

Jasmine meticulously packed for her trip to Canada, folding clothes with care and double-checking her essentials. Excitement mixed with anxiety as she zipped her suitcase, her heart racing at the thought of a new beginning. Her mind buzzed with anticipation, eager to embrace the adventure and leave her past behind.

The Journey to Canada

The journey to Canada was filled with a mix of excitement and apprehension. Jasmine was anxious about meeting her father after so many years and what it would mean for her and her children.

As the plane descended into Canada, Jasmine looked out the window, the sprawling city below her covered in a blanket of snow. She felt a mixture of fear and hope, wondering what awaited them.

At the airport, Jasmine rented a car, and they made their way to Jamal's house. The drive was quiet, the children sensing their mother's tension.

When they arrived, Jasmine took a deep breath and knocked on the door. Jamal opened it, his face a mix of surprise and apprehension.

"Jasmine," he said softly.

"Father," Jasmine replied, her voice trembling.

Cold Reception

Jamal stood nervously scanning the crowd, his eyes finally resting on Jasmine. The resemblance to Nora was striking, and memories came flooding back.

"Come in," Jamal said, his voice stiff. "This is my family."

Jasmine and her kids followed him into the house, where they were met with cold stares and a frosty reception by his wife and four adult children. The atmosphere was cold, and the family's attitude towards Jasmine was distant and unwelcoming, likely influenced by Nora's bad reputation. Undeterred, Jasmine introduced her children, her voice steady but her heart heavy.

"This is my daughter, Amal and my son Elias" There was silence.

Jasmine tried to strike up a conversation with Jamal, hoping to understand why he had never cared about her.

"Father, I just want to know why you never tried to contact me. Why did you leave us?"

Jamal was defensive, his voice hard.

"Your mother... She betrayed me. I couldn't stay. It was too painful."

"But what about me?" Jasmine asked, her voice breaking. "I was just a child."

Jamal looked away, unable to meet her eyes. "It was easier to start over. I'm sorry, Jasmine."

Painful Realization

Jasmine felt a deep sense of sadness and disappointment. The man she had hoped to reconnect with was cold and distant, and his family's attitude mirrored his. She realized there was no chance of a relationship with Jamal. He was still haunted by the past, and she was just a painful reminder.

That night, as they sat in the small guest room, Jasmine hugged Amal and Elias tightly. "We're leaving tomorrow," she whispered. "This was a mistake."

Leaving Canada

The next day, Jasmine packed their bags, her heart heavy with the weight of unmet expectations. They drove back to the airport in silence, each lost in their own thoughts.

As the plane took off, Jasmine looked out the window, the Canadian landscape fading into the distance. She felt alone in the world, despite her eight half-brothers and sisters. Nora had four kids, and Jamal had four kids, but none of them were close to Jasmine. Both parents had instilled hatred in their children about Jasmine, labeling her as the daughter of the bad parent.

Feeling Alone

Back home, Jasmine felt the sting of rejection and isolation. She had hoped for closure, but instead, she found more pain. She wondered how her parents could have poisoned their children against her so thoroughly. The feeling of being alone in the world, despite having family, was overwhelming.

Continuing to Move Forward

Despite the setback, Jasmine refused to let this experience define her. She threw herself back into her work and focused on creating a loving and stable environment for Amal and Elias. She was determined to be the parent she never had, to give her children the love and support that had been denied to her.

Jasmine found solace in her routine, building a sense of normalcy for her family. She continued to devote her life to helping others, finding purpose in her work and joy in watching her children grow.

One evening, as she tucked Amal and Elias into bed, she sat down with a journal and began to write. She poured her heart out, reflecting on her journey and the lessons she had learned.

"Life is full of ups and downs," she wrote. "But it's how we rise after the falls that define us. I may have faced immense pain and betrayal, but I have also found strength and resilience. I have created a life filled with love and purpose, and that is something no one can take away from me."

As Jasmine closed the journal, she felt a sense of peace. She had faced her past and emerged stronger. Her journey was far from over, but she was ready for whatever lay ahead, knowing that she had the strength and resilience to overcome any obstacle.

Jasmine's journey exemplified the power of hope, determination, and the indomitable human spirit. She had crafted a new life rich with love and purpose, and she was prepared to face the future with courage and confidence.

Chapter 6
Stability and Healing

Focusing on Stability

After the painful trip to Canada, Jasmine returned home determined to focus on stability and healing. She wanted to create a secure and loving environment for Amal and Elias, one that would help them thrive despite the turbulence they had experienced.

Every morning, Jasmine woke up early to prepare breakfast for her children. The small kitchen was filled with the smell of pancakes and the sound of laughter as Amal and Elias chatted about their day. Jasmine cherished these moments, feeling a sense of normalcy and peace.

"Mom, can we go to the park after school today?" Elias asked one morning, his eyes shining with excitement.

"Of course, sweetheart," Jasmine replied with a smile. "We'll have a picnic and play some games."

Juggling work and parenting

Balancing work and parenting was a constant challenge for Jasmine. Without any family support, she relied on her own strength and resilience. She worked long hours at her job, often feeling exhausted but determined to provide for her children.

One evening, as Jasmine sat at the kitchen table, reviewing some work documents, Amal approached her.

"Mom, can you help me with my homework?" Amal asked, her voice hesitant.

Jasmine looked up; her eyes tired but filled with love. "Of course, Amal. Let's sit down and do it together."

As they worked through the math problems, Jasmine felt a deep sense of fulfillment. Despite the challenges, she was able to be there for her children and support their growth and development.

Besides their regular schoolwork, Jasmine aimed for her kids to excel academically. She routinely bought books for higher grades and spent time with Amal and Elias, teaching them math, writing, and other subjects. Jasmine referred to this as "extra homework," much to the kids' frequent groans and complaints.

"Mom, do we really have to do more homework?" Elias complained one evening, his eyes pleading for a reprieve.

"Yes, Elias," Jasmine replied firmly but kindly. "It's important to stay ahead. But remember, if you both do well in school, we'll go on vacation this summer."

"Really?" Amal's eyes lit up with excitement.

"Yes, I promise," Jasmine said with a smile. "If you both get good grades, we'll go somewhere fun."

Keeping Her Promises

True to her word, Jasmine kept her promise. When Amal and Elias excelled in their schoolwork, she planned a family vacation. They traveled to various destinations, exploring new places and creating cherished memories.

During their trip to the mountains, Jasmine watched as Amal and Elias played in the snow, their laughter echoing through the crisp air. The sight filled her with joy and a sense of accomplishment. Despite the hardships, she was able to give her children experiences and opportunities that she had never had.

"Thank you, Mom," Amal said one evening as they sat by the fireplace in their cozy cabin. "This is the best vacation ever."

Jasmine hugged her daughter tightly. "You're welcome, sweetheart. I'm so proud of both of you."

Balancing work and parenting was not easy, but Jasmine found ways to make it work. She instilled in her children the value of education and the importance of hard work, all while creating a loving and nurturing environment.

The Struggle of Isolation

However, the struggle of isolation was always present. Jasmine often thought about how her children had no extended family to rely on. If something were to happen to her, who would take care of Amal and Elias? This concern weighed heavily on her mind, especially after the experience with Sam, who had taken advantage of her vulnerability and lack of family support.

One night, as Jasmine lay in bed, she found herself consumed by these thoughts. She felt a pang of loneliness and fear, wondering how she would manage if anything went wrong.

"Stay strong, Jasmine," she whispered to herself. "You have to be there for your children. They need you."

Reflecting on the Past

Jasmine's thoughts often wandered back to her time with Sam. She remembered how he had isolated her, cut her off from friends, and spread rumors about her mental stability. It had been a dark time, and she had felt trapped and alone.

One afternoon, as she sat on the porch watching Amal and Elias play, Jasmine reflected on how far they had come. She had managed to escape Sam's control and create a new life for her family. But the scars of that time still lingered, reminding her of the importance of staying strong and vigilant.

A Serious Concern

The lack of family support was a serious concern for Jasmine. She knew that she couldn't rely on anyone else to help raise her children. This realization made her more determined to build a network of friends and trusted individuals who could be there in times of need.

One day, Jasmine sat down with her friend Leslie, who had been a constant source of support.

"Leslie, I've been thinking a lot about the future," Jasmine said, her voice filled with worry. "If something were to happen to me, who would take care of Amal and Elias? They have no family here."

Leslie reached out and took Jasmine's hand. "Jasmine, you have us. We'll always be here for you and the kids. You're not alone."

Jasmine's eyes filled with tears as she heard Leslie's reassuring words. Overwhelmed with gratitude and relief, she felt a weightlift off her shoulders. A warm smile spread across her face as she embraced the newfound support.

"Thank you, Leslie'"

Building a Support Network

Jasmine felt a sense of relief wash over her. She realized that family didn't always mean blood relations. She could build a support network of friends who would be there for her and her children.

Over the next few months, Jasmine worked on strengthening her connections with friends and neighbors. She attended community events, volunteered at school functions, and tried to be an active part of her children's lives.

One evening, as she stood in the kitchen cooking dinner, she heard a knock on the door. It was her neighbor, Mrs. Patel, who had become a good friend.

"Jasmine, I just wanted to bring over some cookies for the kids," Mrs. Patel said with a warm smile.

"Thank you so much, Mrs. Patel," Jasmine replied, feeling grateful for the kindness and support of her community.

Creating a Sense of Belonging

Jasmine also focused on creating a sense of belonging for Amal and Elias. She wanted them to feel connected to their community and know that they had people they could rely on.

One weekend, Jasmine organized a small gathering at their home, inviting friends and neighbors for a barbecue.

The backyard was filled with laughter and the smell of grilled food. The children played together, and the adults chatted, sharing stories and building bonds.

"Mom, this is so much fun!" Amal said, running up to Jasmine with a big smile on her face.

"I'm glad you're enjoying it, sweetheart," Jasmine replied, hugging her daughter.

Finding Strength in Community

Jasmine found strength in her community and the support of her friends. She realized that she didn't have to face her challenges alone. With the love and support of those around her, she could provide a stable and nurturing environment for her children.

One evening, as she sat on the porch with Leslie, Jasmine felt a sense of peace.

"Leslie, thank you for always being there for us," Jasmine said, her voice filled with gratitude.

"You're family to me, Jasmine," Leslie replied, smiling. "We'll get through this together."

A New Perspective

Jasmine's journey has taught her valuable lessons about resilience, strength, and the importance of community. She had faced immense challenges and had emerged stronger, more determined, and more connected to those around her.

One night, as she tucked Amal and Elias into bed, she felt a deep sense of fulfillment. "Goodnight, my loves," she whispered, kissing their foreheads. "We're going to be okay."

As she closed their bedroom door, Jasmine reflected on the support they had received from their new community, which had become a vital part of their lives. She felt a renewed sense of hope and purpose, knowing they were not alone in their journey. With each passing day, she grew more confident in their ability to build a brighter future.

The Importance of Healing

As the months passed, Jasmine continued to focus on healing and stability. She made time for self-care, seeking therapy to help process the trauma and pain she had experienced. This journey of healing was essential for her well-being and for her ability to be the best mother she could be.

During one therapy session, Jasmine opened up about her fears and concerns.

"I worry about my children and what will happen to them if something happens to me," she said, her voice trembling.

Her therapist nodded. "It's natural to have these concerns, Jasmine. But remember, you are building a strong support network. You are not alone."

The therapist's reassurance gave Jasmine a sense of comfort. She realized that taking steps to heal and build a network of support was not just for her benefit but for her children as well. She began to see the importance of leaning on others and allowing them to help carry some of her burdens. Each therapy session became a steppingstone toward reclaiming her strength and confidence. As she healed, Jasmine noticed positive changes in her children too—they seemed happier and more secure, reflecting the stability she was creating in their lives.

Embracing the Future

Jasmine took the therapist's words to heart. She continued to work on building a sense of security and stability for her family. She enrolled in night classes to further her education and advance her career, determined to provide a better future for Amal and Elias.

One evening, as she sat at the kitchen table studying, Elias came up to her.

"Mom, are you going to school too?" he asked, his eyes filled with curiosity.

"Yes, Elias. I'm taking classes to learn new things and get a better job," Jasmine replied, smiling at her son.

"That's cool! Can I help you study?" Elias asked eagerly.

Jasmine chuckled. "Of course, you can. We can study together."

A New Chapter

A New Jasmine's dedication to her children's future and her own growth was a testament to her strength and resilience. She was determined to create a life filled with love, purpose, and stability for her family.

As the years went by, Amal and Elias flourished in school and in their community. They were surrounded by friends and a support network that Jasmine had carefully built. The fear and uncertainty of the past were replaced by hope and determination.

One evening, as Jasmine watched her children play in the backyard, she felt a sense of pride and accomplishment. She had faced immense challenges and had come out stronger. Her journey was far from over, but she was ready for whatever lay ahead, knowing that she had the strength and resilience to overcome any obstacle

Jasmine's journey highlighted the power of hope, determination, and the unyielding strength of the human spirit. She had created a new life full of love and purpose, and she was prepared to face the future with courage and confidence.

Chapter 7

Blossoming Love and New Beginnings

Meeting Josh

Life for Jasmine had become a delicate balance of work, parenting, and self-discovery. She had built a stable environment for Amal and Elias, ensuring they had the love and support they needed. Yet, despite her focus on her children and career, there was a part of her that yearned for companionship. It was during this time of longing and stability that she met Josh.

It was a sunny afternoon when Jasmine first encountered Josh at a community event. He was tall with a warm smile and an easygoing manner that immediately put her at ease. They struck up a conversation about the event, and Jasmine found herself drawn to his genuine kindness and humor.

"Do you come to these events often?" Josh asked, his eyes twinkling with interest.

"Whenever I can," Jasmine replied with a smile. "It's a great way to feel connected to the community."

As they talked, Jasmine felt a connection forming. Josh was attentive and respectful, qualities that she deeply valued after her tumultuous past with Sam. They exchanged numbers and began seeing each other regularly.

A Blossoming Relationship

Over the next few months, Jasmine and Josh's relationship blossomed. They spent countless evenings talking over dinner, sharing their dreams and experiences. Josh was understanding and supportive, qualities that Jasmine found immensely comforting.

One evening, as they sat on Jasmine's porch watching the sunset, Josh turned to her with a serious expression.

"Jasmine, I've really enjoyed getting to know you and the kids. I care about you a lot," he said, his voice filled with sincerity.

Jasmine's heart fluttered. "I care about you too, Josh."

Their relationship grew deeper with each passing day. Josh was wonderful with Amal and Elias, treating them with kindness and respect. He attended their school events, helped with homework, and became a positive male role model in their lives.

The Proposal

After a year of dating, Josh decided to take their relationship to the next level. He planned a special evening, cooking Jasmine's favorite meal and setting up a candlelit dinner in the backyard. Jasmine was touched by the effort he put into making the night memorable.

As they finished their meal, Josh reached across the table and took Jasmine's hand.

"Jasmine, this past year with you and the kids has been the happiest time of my life," he began, his voice trembling slightly. "I love you, and I love Amal and Elias. I want to spend the rest of my life with you."

Jasmine's eyes filled with tears as Josh got down on one knee and pulled out a small velvet box.

"Jasmine, will you marry me?" he asked, his eyes filled with hope and love.

Overwhelmed with emotion, Jasmine nodded. "Yes, Josh, I will marry you."

They embraced the promise of a future together filling their hearts with joy and anticipation.

A New Beginning

Jasmine and Josh's wedding was a beautiful, intimate ceremony attended by close friends and family. Amal and Elias stood by their mother's side, beaming with happiness. The day was filled with love, laughter, and the promise of a new beginning.

As they exchanged vows, Jasmine felt a profound sense of contentment. She had found a partner who truly cared for her and her children, someone who would stand by her through thick and thin.

"With this ring, I promise to love and cherish you, to support and encourage you, and to build a life filled with love and joy," Josh said, slipping the ring onto Jasmine's finger.

Jasmine repeated the vows, her heart overflowing with love and gratitude. "With this ring, I promise to love and cherish you, to support and encourage you, and to build a life filled with love and joy."

After exchanging their vows, Jasmine and Josh felt a wave of joy and relief wash over them. Tears of happiness glistened in their eyes as they smiled at each other, their hearts full of love and commitment. They embraced tightly, feeling an unbreakable bond, and their friends and family cheered, sharing in their profound moment of unity.

Creating a Stable Home

After the wedding, Jasmine and Josh worked together to create a stable and nurturing home for their family. They moved into a cozy house with a large backyard where the children could play. The house was filled with laughter and warmth, a stark contrast to the turbulence of Jasmine's past.

Josh proved to be a wonderful husband and stepfather. He was patient and attentive, always willing to lend a hand with household chores or help the children with their schoolwork. Jasmine felt a sense of partnership that she had never experienced before.

One evening, as they sat on the couch reading stories to Amal and Elias, Jasmine looked at Josh with gratitude.

"Thank you for being so wonderful with the kids," she said softly.

Josh smiled and kissed her forehead. "They're my family too, Jasmine. I love them as if they were my own."

Family Flourishing

Under Josh's steady presence, the family flourished. Amal and Elias thrived in school and extracurricular activities, their confidence growing with each passing day. Jasmine continued to support their education, often sitting with them to do "extra homework," just as she always had.

"Mom, look! I got an A on my math test!" Elias exclaimed one afternoon, waving his paper in the air.

Jasmine hugged him tightly. "I'm so proud of you, Elias! Keep up the great work."

Amal, too, excelled in her studies and sports, often seeking Josh's advice and guidance. The bond between them grew stronger, and Jasmine felt a deep sense of fulfillment seeing her children happy and secure.

Jasmine's Contentment

Jasmine's life was now filled with love and contentment. She had a supportive husband, flourishing children, and a stable home. She continued to work hard, balancing her career with her responsibilities as a mother and wife.

One day, as she sat in the garden watching the children play, Josh came up behind her and wrapped his arms around her.

"How are you feeling?" he asked, kissing her cheek.

"Content," Jasmine replied, leaning into his embrace. "I finally feel like everything is falling into place."

They sat together, enjoying the peace and tranquility of their home. Jasmine felt a deep sense of gratitude for the life they had built together.

A Future Filled with Hope

As the years went by, Jasmine and Josh continued to build a life filled with love and hope. They supported each other through challenges and celebrated each other's successes. Their home was a sanctuary, a place where love and laughter thrived.

One evening, as they sat by the fireplace, Josh turned to Jasmine with a thoughtful expression.

"Jasmine, I've been thinking about the future. I want us to travel more, to show the kids the world and create new memories together," he said.

Jasmine smiled, her heart swelling with happiness. "That sounds wonderful, Josh. I want that too."

Together, they planned trips and adventures, eager to explore new places and experiences as a family. They traveled to Europe, Hawaii, Africa, and many other destinations, each journey bringing them closer together.

Embracing Life's Journey

Jasmine's journey had been filled with challenges, but she had emerged stronger and more resilient. She had found love and stability, creating a life filled with purpose and joy. Her past no longer defined her; instead, it had shaped her into the person she had become.

One evening, as she watched the sunset with Josh, Amal, and Elias, Jasmine felt a profound sense of peace.

"Life is a journey, filled with ups and downs," she said softly. "But with love and support, we can overcome anything."

Josh squeezed her hand, and the children gathered around, their faces filled with love and admiration.

"We're a family, and we'll always be there for each other," Josh said, his voice filled with conviction.

Jasmine nodded, her heart filled with gratitude. She had found her place in the world, surrounded by love and hope. The future was bright, and she was ready to embrace it with open arms.

Watching her family with a smile, Jasmine knew that they had created something beautiful. A new life filled with purpose and happiness. Together, they would continue to grow, to love, and to embrace the journey of life with hope and joy.

Her journey was far from over, but she faced the future with courage and confidence, knowing that she had the strength to overcome any obstacle.

Chapter 8

Navigating the Challenges

Building a Strong Foundation

Jasmine and Josh focused on building a strong foundation for their family. Their home was a place of love, laughter, and support. Josh's steady presence provided a sense of security, while Jasmine's nurturing nature ensured that Amal and Elias felt cherished and valued.

One evening, as they sat down for dinner, Josh looked around the table and smiled. "I'm so grateful for our family," he said, his voice filled with warmth. "We've built something truly special."

Jasmine reached over and squeezed his hand. "We have, Josh. And I couldn't have done it without you."

Their bond was strong, and together they faced the challenges of parenting and life with resilience and determination.

Traveling as a Family

True to their plans, Jasmine and Josh made traveling a significant part of their family's life. They believed that exploring new places and experiencing different cultures would broaden their children's horizons and create lasting memories.

One summer, they planned a trip to Europe. The excitement was palpable as they packed their bags and prepared for the adventure.

"Mom, I can't wait to see the Eiffel Tower!" Amal exclaimed, her eyes sparkling with anticipation.

"And I want to visit the Colosseum," Elias added, his voice filled with excitement.

As they traveled from Paris to Rome, from London to Athens, Jasmine and Josh reveled in the joy of watching their children discover the world. They visited historic landmarks, sampled local cuisines, and immersed themselves in the rich cultures of each destination.

One evening, as they stood on a hill overlooking the city of Florence, Josh wrapped his arm around Jasmine's shoulders.

"Look at them," he said, nodding towards Amal and Elias, who were admiring the view. "They're so happy."

Jasmine smiled, her heart full. "We're creating memories they'll cherish forever."

Navigating the Teenage Years

As Amal and Elias grew older, they entered the tumultuous teenage years. The once easygoing and cheerful children began to face the challenges of adolescence. While Elias remained relatively easy to manage, Amal's behavior started to change.

One afternoon, Jasmine noticed Amal sitting alone in her room, staring out the window with a distant look in her eyes.

"Amal, is everything okay?" Jasmine asked gently, sitting down beside her daughter.

Amal shrugged, not meeting her mother's gaze. "I'm fine, Mom."

But Jasmine could sense that something was wrong. Amal became increasingly withdrawn and rebellious, often arguing with Jasmine and showing little interest in family activities.

Balancing Family and Work

Balancing family and work became even more challenging for Jasmine. Her job required her to travel one to two days per week, leaving Josh to manage things at home in her absence.

One evening, as Jasmine packed her suitcase for an upcoming trip, she turned to Josh with a worried expression.

"I hate leaving you and the kids, especially with everything going on with Amal," she said, her voice filled with concern.

Josh wrapped his arms around her and kissed her forehead. "Don't worry, Jasmine. We'll manage. You focus on your work, and I'll take care of things here."

While Josh's reassurance helped, Jasmine couldn't shake the feeling of guilt and worry. She knew that Amal needed her, but she also had to fulfill her professional responsibilities.

Teenage Challenges

Amal's rebellion and withdrawal became more pronounced over time. She started spending more time with her friends and less time with her family. Her grades began to slip, and she often came home late without explanation.

One evening, after a particularly heated argument, Amal stormed out of the house, slamming the door behind her. Jasmine felt a pang of helplessness as she watched her daughter walk away.

"What's happening to her, Josh?" Jasmine asked, her voice trembling with emotion. "Why is she pushing us away?"

Josh sighed, his expression troubled. "It's just the teenage years, Jasmine. We'll get through this. We just have to be patient and supportive."

But patience and support were easier said than done. Jasmine struggled to connect with Amal, who seemed determined to shut her out.

The Struggle Continues

Despite their best efforts, the struggle with Amal continued. The once close-knit family dynamic was strained, and Jasmine felt a growing sense of frustration and sadness.

One evening, as she sat in her room, tears streaming down her face, Josh walked in and sat beside her.

"We'll figure this out, Jasmine," he said, his voice gentle. "We'll find a way to help Amal."

Jasmine nodded, wiping away her tears. "I hope so, Josh. I just want her to be happy."

Josh took her hand in his, squeezing it reassuringly. "We might need to try different approaches like new activities, or maybe even talking to other parents who've been through similar situations. Whatever it takes, we'll do it together." Jasmine sighed, feeling a bit of her burden lift. Josh's unwavering support was a beacon of hope in these trying times. They both knew it wouldn't be easy, but their commitment to Amal's well-being and happiness gave them the strength to keep pushing forward.

Seeking Solutions

Determined to find a solution, Jasmine decided to seek professional help for Amal. She researched therapists and counselors who specialized in adolescent behavior and made an appointment for Amal to see a therapist.

One afternoon, as they drove to the therapist's office, Jasmine turned to Amal with a hopeful expression.

"I know things have been tough lately, Amal," she said gently. "But I think talking to someone might help. I want you to be happy and to know that we're here for you."

Amal sighed; her expression wary. "I'll try, Mom. But I don't know if it will help."

Therapy and Healing

The therapy sessions, while a step towards addressing Amal's issues, did not yield the hoped-for results. Amal remained withdrawn and rebellious; her behavior unchanged despite the efforts of the therapist. Jasmine felt a growing sense of frustration but knew she had to stay the course.

One afternoon, Jasmine sat in the therapist's office, her hands clasped tightly in her lap. Dr. Sanders, the therapist, looked at her with a reassuring smile.

"Jasmine, it's important to remember that what Amal is going through is quite common," Dr. Sanders began. "Teenagers often experience anger and rebellion as they try to assert their independence."

"But it's been so difficult," Jasmine replied, her voice tinged with worry. "She's so distant and angry all the time. I'm afraid I'm losing her."

Dr. Sanders nodded empathetically. "I understand your concerns. It's crucial to maintain patience and continue to offer her support. She needs to know that you're there for her, even when she's pushing you away."

Jasmine took a deep breath, trying to absorb the advice. "I just want her to be happy and to feel safe."

"Keep showing her that you care. Sometimes, it takes a while for teenagers to come around. But the foundation of love and support you're providing is what she needs," Dr. Sanders assured her.

Maintaining Patience

Following the session, Jasmine resolved to maintain her patience. She knew it wouldn't be easy, but she was determined to stay strong for Amal. She continued to offer her love and support, even when Amal's behavior tested her limits.

One evening, after yet another argument, Amal stormed into her room and slammed the door. Jasmine stood in the hallway, taking deep breaths to calm herself. She knocked gently on Amal's door.

"Amal, can we talk?" Jasmine asked softly.

There was a long pause before the door opened slightly. Amal's face appeared showing a mix of anger and confusion.

"What is it, Mom?" she asked, her tone defensive.

"I just want you to know that I'm here for you," Jasmine said, her voice steady. "No matter what, I love you, and I want to help you through whatever you're feeling."

Amal looked at her for a moment before nodding slightly. "Okay, Mom."

It wasn't much, but it was a small step towards rebuilding their relationship.

A Glimmer of Hope

Over time, there were moments when Amal seemed to soften. She began to talk to Jasmine more, sharing bits and pieces of her day. These interactions, though brief, gave Jasmine a glimmer of hope.

One afternoon, as they were preparing dinner together, Amal hesitated before speaking.

"Mom, there's this art competition at school," she began, her voice uncertain. "I was thinking of entering."

Jasmine's heart lifted. "That sounds wonderful, Amal! I know you'll do great. Do you need any help with your entry?"

Amal smiled faintly. "Maybe just some supplies. Thanks, Mom."

It was a small moment, but it meant the world to Jasmine. She saw it as a sign that Amal was starting to open up, even if just a little.

Continuing to Move Forward

Jasmine knew the road ahead would still be challenging, but she was committed to moving forward. She focused on maintaining a balance between her responsibilities at work and her role as a mother. Each day brought its own set of challenges, but Jasmine faced them with resilience and determination.

One evening, as she returned home from a business trip, she found Amal and Elias waiting for her with a surprise. They had cooked dinner together, a gesture that filled Jasmine's heart with warmth.

"Welcome home, Mom!" Elias said, hugging her tightly.

"Thanks, Elias," Jasmine replied, her eyes welling up with tears. "This means so much to me."

Amal stood nearby, her expression a mix of shyness and pride. "We wanted to do something nice for you, Mom."

Jasmine hugged her daughter, feeling a deep sense of gratitude. "Thank you, Amal. This is wonderful."

A Stronger Family

Despite the ups and downs, Jasmine saw the progress they were making as a family. They learned to communicate better, support each other, and navigate the complexities of life together. The bond between them grew stronger with each passing day.

One weekend, they decided to go on a family hike. As they walked through the forest, the sunlight filtering through the trees, Jasmine felt a sense of peace.

"Look at this view," Josh said, pointing to the breathtaking landscape before them. "It's amazing."

Amal and Elias nodded in agreement; their faces filled with wonder.

Jasmine smiled, feeling a deep sense of contentment. "We've come a long way, and I'm so proud of all of us."

Josh reached for her hand and squeezed it. "We've built a strong foundation, Jasmine. And we'll continue to grow together."

Embracing the Future

As the years went by, Jasmine and Josh continued to build a life filled with love, purpose, and hope. They faced challenges head-on, supporting each other through the difficult times and celebrating the joyous moments.

Jasmine's job required her to travel, but she always made sure to be present for the important moments in her children's lives. She balanced her career with her responsibilities as a mother and wife, finding fulfillment in both.

One evening, as she returned home from a business trip, she was greeted by the sight of Josh and the kids waiting for her with homemade banners and smiles.

"Welcome home, Mom!" they shouted in unison.

Jasmine's heart swelled with love and gratitude. "It's good to be home," she said, hugging them tightly.

A Promising Path Ahead

Jasmine's journey exemplified the strength of resilience, love, and determination. Despite facing significant hardships, she grew stronger, deepened her family bonds, and looked forward to a brighter future with hope.

As she stood on the porch, watching the sunset with Josh, Amal, and Elias, Jasmine felt a deep sense of peace and contentment.

"Life is a journey, filled with ups and downs," she said softly. "But with love and support, we can overcome anything."

Josh squeezed her hand, and the children gathered around, their faces filled with love and admiration.

"We're a family, and we'll always be there for each other," Josh said, his voice filled with conviction.

Jasmine nodded; her heart filled with gratitude. She had found her place in the world, surrounded by love and hope. The future was bright, and she was ready to embrace it with open arms.

As she stood on the threshold of their home, watching her family with a smile, Jasmine knew that they had created something beautiful. Together, they would continue to grow, to love, and to embrace the journey of life with hope and joy.

Chapter 9

Unraveling Trust and Betrayal

Betrayal and Heartaches

Life had settled into a routine for Jasmine and her family. Amid the daily hustle of work and parenting, Jasmine felt a sense of stability and purpose. However, beneath the surface, seeds of betrayal were beginning to sprout, threatening to upend the delicate balance she had worked so hard to achieve.

Jasmine and Josh's relationship, which had once seemed solid, began to show cracks. Josh's behavior grew increasingly distant and secretive, and Jasmine couldn't shake the feeling that something was amiss. The occasional late nights at work, the hushed phone calls, and the guarded conversations with his coworker all fueled her suspicions. Their once warm and open communication became strained, with Josh often deflecting questions and changing the subject.

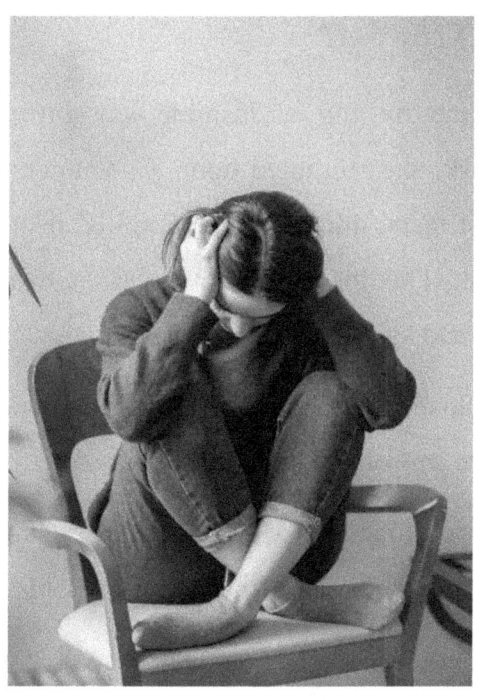

Jasmine noticed that he spent more time away from home, claiming work obligations that seemed more frequent and less plausible. The loving gestures and small acts of kindness that once defined their relationship were replaced with a cold indifference. She couldn't help but wonder if there was more to his relationship with his coworker than he let on. The growing emotional distance left Jasmine feeling isolated and anxious, uncertain about the future of their marriage.

Josh's True Self

One evening, as Jasmine was sorting through some paperwork, she stumbled upon a document that confirmed her worst fears: a loan application that listed their house as collateral. The loan was for Josh's coworker, a woman Jasmine had suspected he was having an affair with.

"Josh, what is this?" Jasmine demanded, waving the document in front of him when he walked through the door.

Josh's face paled as he realized what she had found. "Jasmine, I can explain," he stammered, his voice shaky.

"You can explain?" Jasmine's voice was incredulous. "You're trying to give our house as collateral for your mistress's business loan?"

"It's not what you think," Josh began, but Jasmine cut him off.

"Not what I think? You've been lying to me, sneaking around behind my back, and now you're risking our home for her?" Jasmine's voice trembled with anger and hurt. "How could you do this to us, to the kids?"

Josh looked down, unable to meet her eyes. "I'm sorry, Jasmine. I never meant for it to go this far."

The Confrontation

The confrontation rocked their marriage to its core. Jasmine felt a wave of betrayal and heartache crash over her. She had trusted Josh and believed in the life they were building together, and now it all felt like a lie.

"We need to talk about this," Jasmine said, her voice steadier now but filled with determination. "You need to explain everything."

Over the next few hours, Josh revealed the extent of his betrayal. He admitted to the affair and his sneaky behavior, confessing that he had been trying to help his mistress secure a loan by using their house as collateral. The revelation shattered any remaining trust Jasmine had in him.

"I don't know if I can ever forgive you," Jasmine said quietly, tears streaming down her face. "You've broken something that can't be easily fixed, my trust."

Graduations and New Beginnings

Despite the turmoil at home, Jasmine remained focused on her children. Both Amal and Elias were nearing their high school graduation, and Jasmine was determined to ensure they had a bright future.

One afternoon, Jasmine sat down with Josh to discuss their children's college plans.

"Both Amal and Elias have worked so hard," Jasmine began. "They've earned scholarships that cover their tuition, but they'll need cars to commute to college."

Josh frowned. "I don't think it's a good idea to take on more debt, Jasmine. They can find other ways to get to college."

"I disagree," Jasmine said firmly. "I want them to focus on their studies, not worry about transportation. I'm willing to take on the debt to buy them cars."

Josh shook his head. "It's not practical. They need to learn to be responsible."

"Responsibility doesn't mean struggling unnecessarily," Jasmine retorted. "They've earned these opportunities, and I want to support them."

Despite Josh's opposition, Jasmine went ahead and bought cars for both Amal and Elias, ensuring they could commute to college without any issues.

Jasmine was determined to sacrifice anything for her kids so they could have a better life than hers. She did not want them to struggle as she had, enduring hardships and uncertainties. Jasmine's deepest wish was for her children to experience the life she had always longed for – one filled with opportunities, stability, and happiness. Every decision she made was with their future in mind, ensuring they would never face the same difficulties she had endured.

Choosing a Path

Elias was clear about his future. He had always been focused and driven, knowing exactly what he wanted to study. Amal, on the other hand, was undecided and seemed to drift through her senior year without a clear plan.

One evening, Jasmine sat down with Amal, hoping to help her choose a degree that would lead to a good job.

"Amal, have you thought about what you want to study?" Jasmine asked gently.

Amal shrugged her eyes glued to her phone. "Not really, Mom. I don't know what I want to do."

"That's okay," Jasmine said, trying to be patient. "But we need to start thinking about it. What are you interested in? What subjects do you enjoy?"

Amal sighed. "I don't know, Mom. Josh and his family think I should go into business."

Jasmine's heart sank. "Amal, this is your decision, not theirs. You need to choose something you're passionate about."

But Amal seemed uninterested in her mother's advice, more inclined to listen to Josh and his family. Jasmine sensed that there was something going on between them that she wasn't aware of, and it troubled her deeply.

A Mother's Intuition

Jasmine couldn't shake the feeling that Josh and his family were influencing Amal in ways she didn't understand. She noticed the subtle changes in her daughter's behavior, the way she seemed more distant and secretive.

One evening, as Jasmine was tucking Elias into bed, she decided to confront him about her suspicions.

"Elias, is there something going on between Amal and Josh that I should know about?" Jasmine asked, trying to keep her voice calm.

Elias looked uncomfortable. "I don't know, Mom. Amal doesn't talk to me about it."

"Please, Elias, if you know anything, you have to tell me," Jasmine pleaded.

Elias shook his head. "I'm sorry, Mom. I really don't know."

Jasmine felt a pang of frustration and helplessness. She was in pain, feeling another wave of betrayal as she realized that her children might be keeping secrets from her. The trust she had painstakingly built seemed to be crumbling, and the distance between her and her children grew more pronounced.

Jasmine couldn't help but wonder what had caused this rift and why they felt the need to hide things from her. The thought of losing their closeness weighed heavily on her heart, amplifying her sense of isolation and sorrow.

More Betrayal

One day, after Jasmine returned from work and was handling the finances, she noticed money missing from their joint bank account. Alarmed, she called the bank to investigate and discovered that Josh had withdrawn a significant amount.

When she confronted him that evening, the truth came out.

"I filed for divorce," Josh admitted, his voice devoid of emotion.

Jasmine felt as if the ground had been pulled out from under her. "You did what?" she whispered, her voice trembling.

"I filed for divorce. I can't do this anymore," Josh said, his eyes cold.

"You took money from our account to hire a lawyer behind my back?" Jasmine's voice rose in anger. "How could you do this to me, to our family?"

"You don't divorce someone behind their back; you discuss it together first."

Josh looked away, his expression unreadable. "I just did what I had to do."

Jasmine was overwhelmed with shock and betrayal. Her heart sank, and anger surged through her. She felt blindsided, unable to comprehend how he could make such a drastic decision without even discussing it. The betrayal cut deep, shattering her trust completely.

A Calculated Betrayal

Josh filed for divorce behind Jasmine's back because she held all the debts in her name as the main breadwinner. Handling the finances, Jasmine had nearly paid off the house. Josh's sneaky plan was to escape without any debt, sell the house, and claim his share of the equity, leaving Jasmine buried in financial burdens.

Jasmine was devastated by Josh's betrayal, but she knew she had to stay strong for her children. She began the painful process of reorganizing her finances and preparing for the divorce.

Despite the turmoil, she remained focused on Amal and Elias, supporting them as they transitioned to college. The day both children left for college was bittersweet. Jasmine was proud of their achievements but heartbroken by the fractures in their family.

One evening, as she sat alone in the living room, Jasmine received a call from Amal.

"Mom, I just wanted to let you know that we made it to the dorms safely," Amal said, her voice soft.

"Thank you, Amal. I'm glad to hear that," Jasmine replied, her heart aching.

"Mom... I'm sorry for everything," Amal whispered.

Tears filled Jasmine's eyes. "It's okay, Amal. I love you, no matter what."

As she hung up the phone, Jasmine felt a glimmer of hope. Despite the pain and betrayal, there was still a chance to rebuild her relationship with her children.

Jasmine's journey was far from over, but she was determined to move forward. She would face the future with courage and resilience, knowing that she had the strength to overcome any obstacle.

Jasmine's story exemplified the strength of love and perseverance, serving as a reminder that even in the bleakest moments, there is always hope for a brighter future.

Chapter 10
A New Awakening

Taking control

Jasmine knew she had to take control of her life. She couldn't rely on someone who had betrayed her trust so profoundly. She began to reevaluate their marriage and her future. She had been handling all the household finances because she earned more money than Josh. Most of the debts were in her name, and she realized how vulnerable that made her.

"Josh, I've been handling everything," Jasmine said one night, her voice calm but firm. "The bills, the mortgage, the kids' expenses—it's all on me. And you thought you could just walk away and leave me buried in debt?"

"I didn't think it through," Josh admitted, his voice barely above a whisper.

"Well, you need to start thinking," Jasmine replied. "Because I'm seeking legal advice. I can't trust you anymore."

Change of heart

Josh's admission and Jasmine's resolve to seek legal advice marked a turning point. Jasmine knew she had to protect herself and her children. She began rearranging the finances, consolidating debts, and making sure everything was in order. She wanted to buy time to prepare for the inevitable divorce.

During this time, Josh had a change of heart and canceled the divorce proceedings. He tried to mend their relationship, but Jasmine's trust was irrevocably broken.

Elias tried to convince Jasmine not to file for divorce, pleading with her to reconsider. However, Jasmine had lost all trust in him. The betrayal and deceit she had endured were too much to overlook. She remained resolute, knowing that her decision was necessary to reclaim her sense of security and peace.

One evening, as they sat at the kitchen table, Jasmine broached the subject again. "Josh, I think we need to move forward with the divorce."

Josh looked at her, his expression pained. "Are you sure, Jasmine? I thought we were trying to work things out."

"I can't trust you anymore," Jasmine said, her voice heavy with sadness. "But I want to do this amicably, for the sake of the kids. We need to keep a good relationship with them."

An Amicable Divorce

Jasmine and Josh collaborated to arrange an amicable divorce, agreeing on financial matters and maintaining a cordial relationship to minimize the impact on Amal and Elias. Despite the pain and betrayal, Jasmine remained determined to provide a stable environment for her children. Her primary focus was on ensuring their well-being and maintaining a sense of normalcy during the transition.

By that time, both kids were living in college dorms. Amal had become increasingly distant, preferring to spend her holidays with Josh and his family. She often went straight from college to their house, leaving Jasmine feeling isolated and hurt.

One afternoon, Jasmine decided to call Amal, hoping to bridge the gap between them.

"Amal, I miss you," Jasmine began softly. "I wish you would spend more time here."

Amal's voice was distant. "I just feel more comfortable at Dad's."

"I understand," Jasmine said, her voice trembling. "But remember, I'm always here for you, no matter what."

Elias, on the other hand, maintained a good relationship with Jasmine. He took turns spending the holidays with both parents, trying to keep the peace. Jasmine cherished the time she had with him, finding solace in their bond.

Building a New Life

As the divorce proceedings finalized, Jasmine focused on building a new life for herself and her children. She continued to work hard, balancing her career with her responsibilities as a mother. She continued to help her kids financially with their college and living expenses.

One evening, as she sat with Elias, he asked her a question that made her pause.

"Mom, are you okay?" Elias asked, his eyes filled with concern.

Jasmine smiled, touched by his worry. "I'm okay, Elias. It's been hard, but we're getting through it."

"You know, you can always talk to me," Elias said, his voice gentle.

"Thank you, sweetheart," Jasmine replied, hugging him tightly. "I love you so much."

Facing Challenges Together

Despite the challenges, Jasmine and her children continued to move forward. They faced each day with resilience and hope, finding strength in their bond. Jasmine knew that the road ahead would not be easy, but she was determined to navigate it with grace and courage.

One weekend, Elias came home from college to spend time with Jasmine. They decided to go on a camping trip, hoping to create new

memories and strengthen their bond. Sitting by the campfire, roasting marshmallows, they shared stories and laughter, enjoying the chance to reconnect amidst nature's tranquility. Elias turned to her with a thoughtful expression.

"Mom, do you ever think about the future?" he asked.

"All the time," Jasmine replied, her eyes reflecting the flickering flames. "But I'm learning to take it one day at a time."

Elias nodded, a smile playing on his lips. "I think we're going to be okay."

Jasmine felt a surge of love for her son. "I know we will be, Elias. We have each other, and that's what matters."

Embracing New Beginnings

As the months passed, Jasmine embraced her new life. She found joy in the small moments, like her phone conversations with Elias and the peace of her home. Each day brought new opportunities for growth and healing. Her resilience was evident in her unwavering dedication to creating a positive environment for her kids.

Jasmine continued to work hard, ensuring that Amal and Elias had everything they needed to succeed. She was determined to provide them with the stability and support they deserved. Her efforts were paying off, as she watched them thrive academically and personally. Their happiness became her greatest reward, filling her with a sense of accomplishment.

One evening, as she sat on the porch, watching the sunset, Jasmine felt a sense of contentment. The sky's colors mirrored the hope she felt within. Despite the pain and betrayal she had endured, she had found a way to move forward. In those quiet moments, she realized that her strength and love for her children were the foundations of her newfound happiness.

Hopes for a Bright Future

Jasmine's journey exemplified resilience and determination. Despite facing immense challenges, she emerged stronger and more focused on her future. She built a life filled with love and purpose, creating a stable and nurturing environment for her children.

As she stood on the porch, watching the stars twinkle in the night sky, she felt a sense of peace. She knew that the future held many uncertainties, but she was ready to face them with courage and grace.

Her story exemplified the power of love and resilience, serving as a reminder that hope exists even in the darkest times. Jasmine discovered her strength and faced life's journey with an open heart and unwavering determination.

Chapter 11
A Mother's Despair

Estrangement with Amal

Jasmine couldn't understand why Amal's behavior had changed so drastically. Despite her best efforts to reconnect with her daughter, Amal remained distant and cold. It seemed that the bond they once shared had been severed, replaced by a wall of silence and hostility.

One evening, as Jasmine sat alone in her living room, she picked up the phone and dialed Amal's number, hoping to bridge the gap between them.

"Hello?" Amal's voice was flat and uninterested.

"Amal, it's Mom," Jasmine said, trying to keep her voice steady. "I wanted to talk to you about what's been going on."

Amal sighed audibly. "What is there to talk about, Mom?"

Jasmine was heartbroken and confused by Amal's distant and unexplained behavior. Despite her efforts to bridge the gap, she sensed an impenetrable wall between them. Knowing Josh's sneaky nature, Jasmine began to suspect that he had done something to alienate Amal from her. The realization gnawed at her, fueling her determination to uncover the truth and mend their fractured relationship.

Graduation Heartbreak

On the day of Amal's graduation, Amal invited Josh and his family but excluded Jasmine. The mother who has been there for her since the day she was born. Jasmine sat in her living room, trying to keep her emotions in check. She knew that Josh and his family would be there, and the thought of them celebrating her daughter's achievements without her was almost too much to bear.

Jasmine felt a profound sense of betrayal and heartbreak, recognizing Josh and his family's manipulative influence over Amal. During a strained conversation with Amal, Jasmine could sense the unexplained hatred in her daughter's voice, a painful realization of the deep divide that had been created between them.

"Why have you been so distant? Why didn't you invite me to your graduation?" Jasmine's voice trembled with emotion.

"Because, Mom," Amal replied coldly, "I didn't want any drama. Josh and his family were there for me. You just don't get it."

Jasmine's heart sank. "But I've always been there for you, Amal. I've supported you in everything."

There was a long pause before Amal spoke again. "I have to go, Mom. Goodbye."

Jasmine was left holding the phone, tears streaming down her face. The realization that she had not been invited to Amal's graduation was a crushing blow. She had worked tirelessly to support her children, paying for their college expenses, buying them cars, and ensuring they had every opportunity to succeed. Yet, when the moment of celebration came, she was left out.

A Mother's Resilience

Determined not to give up, Jasmine decided to reach out to Amal again. She hoped to find out what was going on between Josh, Amal, and his family. She dialed Amal's number once more, bracing herself for another difficult conversation.

"Hi, Amal. It's Mom again," Jasmine began, her voice filled with a mix of hope and desperation.

"Mom, I told you, there's nothing to talk about," Amal replied, her tone cold and unyielding.

"Amal, please. I just want to understand why things have changed between us. What have I done to make you so distant?" Jasmine pleaded.

"You haven't done anything, Mom," Amal said flatly. "I just don't want to talk about it."

Jasmine felt a pang of frustration and sorrow. "But Amal, I'm your mother. I love you. Can't we work this out?"

"Goodbye, Mom," Amal said, and the line went dead.

Jasmine felt a profound sense of loss and desperation, overwhelmed by frustration as she grappled with Amal's unexplained distance. She was determined to uncover the truth, suspecting Josh's manipulation. Her longing to reconnect with her daughter was matched only by her resolve to understand the betrayal that had driven them apart.

Moving Away

Both Amal and Elias graduated college with honors, a milestone that filled Jasmine with pride. However, despite her hopes that they would find jobs close to home, both kids accepted positions out of state. The physical distance only seemed to widen the emotional gap between them and their mother. Jasmine couldn't shake the feeling that Josh and his family were influencing her children, subtly encouraging them to keep their distance.

The sense of isolation grew stronger with each passing day, as did Jasmine's suspicion that there was a deliberate effort to turn her children against her. This gnawed at her, making her question everything she knew about her family dynamics. The more she thought about it, the more she felt an overwhelming need to understand what had gone wrong and why her relationship with Amal and Elias had deteriorated so drastically.

Uncovering Hidden Influences

Elias had been working out of state, and Jasmine had noticed a change in him and a growing distance between them. Elias seemed to be in a rush to get off the phone whenever Jasmine asked about Amal or what was going on behind her back. She sensed that something was wrong and was determined to find out the truth.

It was very difficult for Jasmine, who felt like there was a conspiracy forming against her.

Determined to get to the bottom of things, Jasmine decided to confront Elias. She dialed his number.

"Hi Elias, it's Mom" her heart pounding with anticipation.

"Hi, Mom," Elias answered, his voice sounding tired.

"How was work today?" Jasmine asked, trying to keep the conversation light.

"It was fine. Just busy," Elias replied, his tone clipped.

Jasmine took a deep breath. "Elias, I've been feeling like there's something going on that you're not telling me. You've been so distant lately."

There was a long pause on the other end of the line before Elias finally spoke. "Mom, it's complicated."

"What's so complicated about it?" Jasmine demanded gently. "I deserve to know the truth. Why are you and Amal so distant? Why is Josh and his family so involved in your lives?"

After a long silence, Elias sighed heavily. "Mom, when I had a relationship with you, Josh and Amal stopped talking to me. I just got my relationship back with them."

Jasmine's heart felt like it was being ripped apart. "Elias, I love you. I'm your mother. Why can't we all just be together?"

"I can't talk about this anymore, Mom," Elias said, his voice strained. "Goodbye."

Before Jasmine could respond, the line went dead. She was left staring at the phone, tears streaming down her face. The realization that her children were being manipulated against her was a crushing blow.

A Mother's Despair

Jasmine's reaction to the betrayal and the many unanswered questions was one of deep sorrow and confusion. Nobody was willing to talk, leaving Jasmine to feel like her world was collapsing around her. She had always been there for her children, providing for them, supporting them, and loving them unconditionally. Now, she felt like an outsider, excluded from their lives by the very people who should have been family.

Jasmine sat in her living room, staring at the walls, feeling a profound sense of despair. The silence in the house was deafening, a stark contrast to the laughter and love that once filled the space. Memories of happier times haunted her, amplifying her loneliness. She replayed moments in her mind, searching for signs she might have missed, clues that could explain the sudden distance.

The betrayal stung even more as she thought about Josh's manipulations and the influence he seemed to hold over her children. The questions with no answers tormented her, making it hard to find any peace or solace. Jasmine's heart ached for the bond she once shared with Amal and Elias, leaving her yearning for reconciliation and understanding.

A Mother's Heartbreak and Loss

Jasmine felt her world collapsing around her as her children, who were her entire life, seemed distant and estranged. She had lived for them, sacrificing everything to ensure they had a better life than she did. The sense of loss was overwhelming, as the bond she cherished with them appeared to be slipping away.

Her children were the only family Jasmine had, representing her hope for a close-knit future. Now, that hope had been ripped away, leaving her feeling isolated and heartbroken. The sacrifices she made for their happiness and well-being felt in vain, and the pain of their absence was a constant, gnawing ache in her heart.

Determined To Fight for Her Kids

Despite the overwhelming sense of betrayal and loss, Jasmine refused to give up. She continued to reach out to her children, hoping to rebuild the bridges that had been burned. She called, texted, and emailed them, but received no responses. Each unanswered message deepened her heartache.

One afternoon, she sent another message to Amal, her fingers trembling as she typed.

"Amal, it's Mom. I miss you so much. Please talk to me. I just want to understand what's happening. I love you."

Days passed with no reply. Jasmine tried calling again, only to be met with a voicemail each time. The silence was crushing, a constant reminder of the distance that had grown between them.

Resolute in Seeking Answers

Determined not to give up, Jasmine embarked on a quest to seek answers. She reached out to friends, family, and anyone who might have insight into what was happening. Yet, no one seemed to know the full story. The pieces of the puzzle remained scattered, leaving Jasmine in a state of confusion and heartache.

One evening, as she sat alone, she received a text message from an old friend: "Hey, Jasmine. I heard about what's been going on. I'm here if you need to talk." Jasmine felt a glimmer of hope. She replied quickly, setting up a meeting with her friend, hoping to gain some clarity and support.

As she waited for the meeting, Jasmine reflected on her journey. She had faced immense challenges, from her tumultuous relationship with Josh to the estrangement from her children. Yet, through it all, she had remained strong, determined to find a way forward.

Jasmine's resolve was unwavering, and the possibility of finally uncovering the truth brought her a renewed sense of purpose. She knew that this meeting could be a turning point in her search for answers and hoped it would lead her closer to mending the fractured bonds with her children.

A Glimmer of Hope

When Jasmine met her friend for coffee, she poured out her heart, sharing the pain and confusion she had been experiencing. Her friend listened patiently, offering words of comfort and support.

"Jasmine, you're one of the strongest people I know," her friend said, squeezing her hand. "You've been through so much, and you're still standing. Don't give up on finding the truth. Keep reaching out to your children. They need to know how much you love them."

As they continued talking, her friend provided valuable insights and offered to help Jasmine reconnect with her children. They discussed potential strategies and ways to approach the situation delicately, so as not to push Amal and Elias further away. Jasmine felt a renewed sense of determination. She knew the road ahead would be difficult, but she was ready to face it with courage and resilience.

Her friend's encouragement was like a lifeline, giving Jasmine the strength she needed to move forward. She left the café with a clear mind and a heart full of hope. That evening, Jasmine sat down and penned heartfelt letters to Amal and Elias, expressing her love and desire to understand what had gone wrong. She was prepared to fight for her family, no matter how long it took.

A Mother's Love

Jasmine's journey was far from over, but she approached the future with determination and hope. Her unwavering love for her children drove her to do whatever it took to show them how much she cared. One evening, as she sat on the porch watching the sunset, she felt a profound sense of peace. Despite facing immense challenges and heartbreak, she discovered her own strength and resilience.

Her story exemplified the power of love and determination, serving as a reminder that even in the darkest times, there is always hope for a brighter tomorrow. Jasmine knew she would continue to fight for her children, seek the answers she needed, and build a future filled with love and joy. As she stood up and walked back into the house, she felt a renewed sense of purpose, ready to face whatever challenges lay ahead, confident in her strength to overcome them.

Jasmine's journey was a testament to the power of a mother's love—a force that could withstand any storm and shine through even the darkest clouds.

Chapter 12
A Life of Questions and Despair

Financial Burdens and Estrangement

The divorce and the kids' departure left Jasmine buried in debt. She had taken on significant financial burdens, from college expenses to the cost of buying cars for Amal and Elias. Without Josh's support and with her children estranged, the weight of these responsibilities fell squarely on her shoulders. She felt overwhelmed by the sheer magnitude of her financial obligations, unsure of how she would manage to keep everything afloat.

The Daily Struggles

Every day was a struggle. Jasmine worked tirelessly to pay off the debts, juggling multiple jobs to make ends meet. She took on every opportunity, no matter how grueling, to ensure she could meet her financial commitments. Each day began before dawn and ended late at night, her energy drained but her determination unwavering.

Despite her relentless efforts, it felt like an uphill battle, with the debts looming over her like a dark cloud. Her once vibrant spirit was weighed down by the relentless pressure. The stress took a toll on her health, and moments of joy were overshadowed by financial worries. Yet, Jasmine refused to give up, driven by the hope of a brighter future.

Unanswered Questions

But no matter how hard she worked, the questions gnawed at her, questions that had no easy answers. What had happened behind her back? How had Josh manipulated their children so effectively? Each unanswered question added to her emotional burden, leaving her feeling betrayed and confused. The sense of betrayal felt like a nightmare that wouldn't go away, haunting her thoughts and dreams, making it difficult to find peace.

The nights were the worst, filled with restless hours of tossing and turning, her mind racing with relentless thoughts. She replayed every interaction, every conversation, searching for clues she might have missed. Jasmine couldn't shake the feeling that there were deeper, darker truths yet to be uncovered. This constant mental torment left her exhausted, both physically and emotionally.

Her friends noticed the change in her, the once vibrant and cheerful Jasmine was now overshadowed by worry and sorrow. They offered their support, but Jasmine felt isolated in her struggle as if no one could truly understand the depth of her pain. She appreciated their concern, yet the unanswered questions created a barrier that kept her from fully opening up. In her quiet moments, she resolved to keep fighting for answers, no matter how elusive they seemed.

The Pain of Betrayal

Jasmine's heart ached with the realization that the people she had trusted the most had turned against her. The betrayal was a wound that refused to heal, constantly reopened by the memories of her children and the life she had once envisioned. It felt as though the rug had been pulled from under her feet, leaving her in a freefall of confusion and despair. Each memory was a reminder of what she had lost, deepening the sense of loneliness and heartbreak.

Despite the pain, she remained determined to seek the truth and understand how everything had gone so wrong. Her journey was far from over, but she faced it with resilience and a flicker of hope that one day, she might find the answers she so desperately sought. Jasmine's resolve grew stronger with each passing day, fueled by the love she still held for her children. She knew that giving up was not an option, and that perseverance was her only path to healing and understanding.

Relentless Doubts and Realizations

As Jasmine reflected on the past, she began to see things in a new light. The signs of Josh's manipulations had been there, but she had missed them. She remembered Amal's teenage rebellion, which she had dismissed as a typical phase. But now, she wondered if there had been more to it.

Sitting alone in her living room, Jasmine's thoughts spiraled. "What if Josh abused Amal?" she thought, her heart racing. The idea was horrifying, but the more she considered it, the more plausible it seemed. Josh had always been sneaky, always hiding things. Was it possible he had hidden something so monstrous? The thought sent chills down her spine, making her feel both furious and helpless.

"Who did I marry?" Jasmine whispered to herself, her voice trembling. "Is he a pedophile who disguised himself as a loving stepfather and husband?" The possibility gnawed at her, creating a storm of emotions within her. She felt a mixture of anger, fear, and sorrow. Her mind raced with the potential implications of such a revelation. How could she have missed the signs? What else had he been hiding? Jasmine's trust in her own judgment wavered as she grappled with these dark thoughts.

As the night wore on, Jasmine's desperation grew. She realized she needed answers, not only to understand what had happened to her family but to protect her children. She resolved to dig deeper, to uncover the truth no matter how painful it might be. Reaching out to Amal seemed more urgent than ever, and Jasmine knew she had to approach it with care, ensuring she didn't push her further away. Her mind churned with plans and questions, each one reinforcing her determination to uncover the truth.

A Mother's Desperate Search for Answers

Jasmine called Amal, her voice trembling. "Amal, has Josh ever done anything to you when I wasn't around? At any time?" Silence lingered before Amal sharply replied,

"No, Mom. Nothing happened," and abruptly hung up. Jasmine's heart raced, and her mind swirled with worry and doubt. She desperately needed answers.

Desperate, Jasmine reached out to her friend Leslie. "Can you call Amal and see if she'll open up to you?" Jasmine pleaded. Leslie agreed, sensing the urgency in her friend's voice. After a tense wait, Leslie called back. "Amal said she doesn't want you to ask any questions about the past."

Jasmine felt overwhelming frustration because she knew Amal was hiding something. Her mind raced with possibilities and fears, unsure of what to believe. The uncertainty gnawed at her, making it hard to focus on anything else. She knew she needed to tread carefully, but the lack of clarity left her feeling helpless and anxious.

Isolation and Despair

The relentless doubts and isolation took a toll on Jasmine's mental health. She fell into a deep depression, feeling more alone than ever. Her life, which had once been filled with hope and the joy of her children, now felt like a series of betrayals and heartbreaks.

Jasmine's depression grew worse. She struggled to get out of bed in the morning, her motivation sapped by the overwhelming weight of her despair. Her job performance suffered, and eventually, she lost her job. The loss of her income only added to her stress, pushing her deeper into a dark place.

One night, the despair became too much to bear. Jasmine sat on the edge of her bed, contemplating suicide. "Maybe it would be easier if I just ended it," she thought, tears streaming down her face. The pain of her past, the betrayal of her children, and the relentless financial strain seemed too much to handle.

Destined to Walk This Journey Alone?

As she sat there, Jasmine wondered if she was destined to walk this journey alone. Her life had been filled with pain and agony: a rough childhood with a revengeful mother, selfish parents who had abandoned her, abusive and deceitful husbands, and now, estrangement from her children. Each memory pierced her heart, deepening the sense of isolation that enveloped her.

Her life seemed like walking through a jungle all alone, constantly falling and getting back up. She kept asking herself why she was destined to have such a hard life from the beginning. Every step forward seemed to bring new obstacles, testing her resilience and strength. The weight of her struggles bore down on her, making each day a battle for survival and sanity.

"Why me?" she whispered into the darkness. "What did I do to deserve this?" The unanswered question echoed in the silence, amplifying her sense of despair. Jasmine longed for a reprieve, a sign that her suffering had meaning or an end in sight. Yet, despite the overwhelming challenges, a flicker of hope remained, urging her to keep moving forward, to find a reason to believe that better days were possible.

Blaming Herself

As she processed her emotions, Jasmine couldn't help but blame herself. The guilt was a heavy burden, one that compounded her existing pain and made it difficult to move forward. She felt she should have seen what was happening and should have protected her children better. Each memory of the past mistakes weighed on her heart, intensifying her sense of failure.

"I should have known," she whispered to herself, tears streaming down her face. "I should have seen the signs. I let them down." Her voice trembled with regret, echoing in the silent room. The words hung in the air, a stark reminder of the weight she carried. Jasmine's self-reproach was relentless, making her question her ability to ever truly heal and find peace.

Seeking Strength in Solitude

Despite the overwhelming despair, something inside Jasmine refused to give up. She thought about her children and the love she still had for them, even if they were distant. She thought about the dreams she once had, the strength she had shown in the past, and the resilience that had carried her through so many trials.

Slowly, Jasmine began to rebuild her life. She sought therapy, determined to address the deep-seated pain and trauma that had been haunting her. Her therapist, a kind and understanding woman named Dr. Nguyen, helped her navigate the tangled web of her emotions.

In one of their sessions, Jasmine finally voiced her deepest fears. "What if Josh abused Amal?" she asked, her voice barely above a whisper.

"Jasmine, you did the best you could with the information you had," Dr. Nguyen reassured her. "It's not your fault."

Dr. Nguyen looked at her with compassionate eyes. "Jasmine, it's important to focus on what you can control. We may never know the full truth, but we can work on healing you."

Seeking Justice and Understanding

Jasmine's desire for justice and understanding grew stronger. She wanted to know the truth about what had happened behind her back. She reached out to legal advisors and considered reopening old wounds to find out if there was any way to bring Josh to justice if he had indeed harmed her children.

However, the legal advisors told her the same thing: without concrete evidence and with Amal refusing to speak, it would be nearly impossible to prove anything.

"Ms. Jasmine, we understand your concerns, but without more evidence, there's not much we can do," one advisor told her gently.

The roadblocks only added to Jasmine's frustration and helplessness. How could she seek justice when the truth seemed so elusive?

Finding Purpose Again

Jasmine took Dr. Nguyen's words to heart. She knew she needed to find a purpose again, something to anchor her in the storm of her emotions. Determined to create a positive change, she threw herself into volunteer work, finding solace in helping others. She started working with a local animal rescue organization, channeling her energy into caring for animals who needed love and support.

The work brought her a sense of peace she hadn't felt in years. Each day at the shelter, Jasmine found herself smiling more and worrying less. The animals, with their unconditional love and trust, reminded her that there was still goodness in the world. Their simple joy in her presence gave her a reason to get up in the morning, a purpose that went beyond her own pain.

As she bonded with the animals, Jasmine's heart began to heal. She realized that by helping them, she was also helping herself. The connections she formed with the rescued animals gave her a renewed sense of hope and fulfillment. Every wagging tail and purr of contentment reinforced her belief in second chances. Slowly, she started to envision a future where her past sorrows were replaced with new beginnings and brighter days.

Endless Longing

Jasmine spent holidays, birthdays, and Mother's Day alone, with no contact from her kids. Despite the challenges, she never stopped longing for them. She missed their laughter, their presence, and the bond they once shared. The longing was a constant ache, a poignant reminder of what she had lost and a void that nothing else could fill.

She continued to send messages, hoping for a response. She called, texted, and emailed, but received no answers. Each silence deepened her heartache, yet she refused to give up hope. The absence of replies was like a cold wind blowing through her life, but her love for her children remained steadfast and unwavering.

One evening, as she sat on her porch watching the sunset, she whispered into the twilight, "Amal, Elias, I miss you. I love you. Please come back to me." The fading light mirrored her sense of longing, each word carrying the weight of her heartache and hope. Despite the silence, she held onto the belief that one day, her children would hear her call and return to her waiting arms.

Chapter 13
Embracing a Solitary Path

Losing Trust in Humanity

The betrayals and heartbreaks had left Jasmine deeply scarred. She found it impossible to trust anyone again, the wounds too fresh and too deep. Every interaction with people seemed tainted by doubt and suspicion. She couldn't help but wonder if they too would betray her eventually. Her once open and hopeful heart had turned into a fortress, guarded and wary.

Jasmine made a conscious decision to close herself off from the world. She refused to allow anyone new into her life, fearing further heartbreak and deceit. The isolation was both a comfort and a curse, providing her with the peace she desperately craved but also a constant reminder of the loneliness that had taken root in her soul.

Living with Doubt

The doubts and unanswered questions about her past, about Josh and her children, continued to haunt her. Every quiet moment was an opportunity for her mind to wander back to those dark places, questioning everything she thought she knew. Did Josh start manipulating the kids when they were younger? What other things did he do behind my back that I didn't notice? Was there more to his behavior than she realized? These questions swirled in her mind, refusing to be silenced.

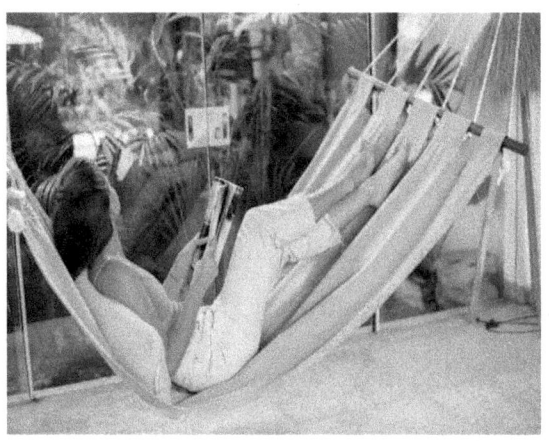

Despite the doubts, Jasmine found a strange sense of peace in her solitude. She no longer had to worry about the intentions of others, and no longer had to guard herself against betrayal. Her life had become a sanctuary of sorts, a place where she could focus on her own healing and growth.

Finding Peace and Safety with Her Dogs

Jasmine found solace in the company of her two rescued dogs, Max and Bella. They were her faithful companions, offering unconditional love and loyalty in a world that had shown her little of either. The dogs became her family, providing a sense of security and belonging that she had longed for. Their presence in her life was a constant reminder that love and loyalty still existed.

Every morning, Jasmine would take Max and Bella for a walk in the park.

The fresh air and the simple joy of watching her dogs play brought a sense of peace to her troubled mind. She cherished those moments when the worries of the world seemed to fade away. The playful antics of Max and Bella often made her smile, providing a much-needed distraction from her thoughts.

The dogs seemed to understand her pain, offering comfort in their own quiet way. Max would rest his head on her lap, while Bella would curl up beside her, their warmth and closeness soothing her aching heart. Jasmine realized that, in their own way, they were healing her wounds. Their unwavering companionship and gentle affection gave her the strength to face each day, reminding her that she was not alone in her journey.

Solace in Small Things

Jasmine began to find comfort in the small things. The simple pleasures of life, like a warm cup of tea on a cold morning, the sound of rain tapping against her window, or the feel of the sun on her face during her walks with Max and Bella, became sources of comfort and joy. She learned to appreciate these moments, finding peace in their simplicity.

Her animal rescue work also brought her a sense of purpose. Each animal she helped was a reminder that she could still make a positive impact in the world, even if her own life felt shattered. The animals she cared for became symbols of hope and resilience, their stories of survival inspiring her to keep moving forward. This sense of purpose rekindled her spirit, giving her a reason to get up each day.

Jasmine found peace in the bonds she formed with the animals she rescued. Each furry friend brought unique challenges and rewards, teaching her valuable lessons in patience and empathy. The love she gave and received in return was a healing balm for her soul, mending the broken parts of her heart. In these connections, she found the strength to rebuild her life, one small act of kindness at a time.

Hoping for Reconciliation

Despite her decision to close herself off from others, Jasmine never gave up hope for reconciliation with her children. She continued to send messages, letters, and emails, hoping that one day Amal and Elias would respond. Each unanswered message was a reminder of the distance between them, but she refused to give up hope.

"Dear Amal and Elias," she wrote in one of her letters. "I miss you both every day. I hope you are well and happy. Please know that I love you more than words can express. I'm here, always waiting, always hoping for the day we can be together again. Love, Mom."

Embracing a New Path

Jasmine knew she had to find a way to move forward, to embrace a new path despite the pain and loneliness. She set new goals for herself, focusing on her own growth and well-being. She decided to pursue further education, enrolling in online courses that allowed her to study from the safety of her home.

Her studies provided a new sense of purpose, a way to channel her energy into something positive. She found joy in learning new things, expanding her horizons, and challenging herself academically. The pursuit of knowledge became a source of strength and empowerment.

Finding a New Job

With her newfound education, Jasmine sought out new job opportunities. She eventually found a position at a local non-profit organization that focused on animal welfare.

The job was a perfect fit, allowing her to combine her love for animals with her professional skills.

Working at the non-profit brought a sense of fulfillment that she had been missing. She felt valued and appreciated, her efforts making a tangible difference in the lives of the animals she cared for. The work was demanding but rewarding, giving her a sense of purpose and direction.

A Life of Reflection

Jasmine spent a lot of time reflecting on her journey. She thought about the trials she had faced, the people who had hurt her, and the lessons she had learned along the way. Her life had been a series of ups and downs, filled with moments of joy and sorrow, hope and despair.

As she reflected, Jasmine began to see her experiences in a new light. She realized that each challenge had shaped her, teaching her valuable lessons about resilience, strength, and the importance of self-love. She learned to forgive herself for the mistakes she had made, understanding that she had done the best she could with the information she had at the time.

Embracing the Journey

Despite the hardships, Jasmine learned to embrace her journey. She understood that life was not about avoiding pain but about finding the strength to move through it. She learned to appreciate the beauty in her struggles, recognizing that they had made her the person she is today.

One evening, as she sat on her porch with Max and Bella by her side, Jasmine felt a sense of peace. The sun was setting, casting a warm golden glow over the landscape. She watched as the sky turned shades of pink and orange, a reminder of the beauty that could be found even in the darkest times.

She thought about her children, hoping that one day they would find their way back to her. But she also knew that she couldn't live her life waiting for that day to come. She had to keep moving forward, embracing each moment and finding joy in the journey.

A New Beginning

Jasmine's story was one of resilience and hope. She had faced immense challenges but had found the strength to rise above them. Her journey was far from over, but she was ready to face whatever came next with courage and grace.

As she stood up and walked back into the house, she felt a renewed sense of purpose. She was ready to embrace her new path, knowing that she had the strength to overcome any obstacle. Her life was not defined by the betrayals and heartbreaks she had faced but by the love and resilience that had carried her through.

Jasmine's journey was a testimony to the strength of the human spirit, a reminder that even in the darkest times, there is always hope for a brighter tomorrow. She knew that she would continue to fight for her children, to seek the answers she needed, and to build a future filled with love and joy.

As she looked ahead, Jasmine felt a sense of peace. She had found her strength, her purpose, and her place in the world. She was ready to face whatever challenges lay ahead, knowing that she had the resilience to find happiness and fulfillment.

Conclusion

A Journey of Resilience and Hope

Jasmine's journey was a testament to the unyielding strength of the human spirit. Despite the myriad of challenges she faced—betrayal, heartbreak, and the painful estrangement from her children—she never lost sight of her inner resilience. Her life was a tapestry woven with threads of love, pain, joy, and sorrow, each experience shaping her into a woman of profound strength and compassion.

Through the darkest of times, Jasmine found solace in the simplest of pleasures. Her two rescued dogs, Max and Bella, became her steadfast companions, offering unconditional love and comfort. Her work with the local animal rescue organization brought purpose and fulfillment, allowing her to make a tangible difference in the lives of those who needed it most.

Jasmine's reflections on her life brought clarity and acceptance. She understood that her journey was not about avoiding pain but about finding the courage to confront it, to heal, and to grow. Each challenge she faced was a lesson in resilience, teaching her the importance of self-love and the power of hope.

Despite the distance and silence from her children, Jasmine never gave up hope for reconciliation. Her love for Amal and Elias remained unwavering, a beacon of light guiding her through the darkest moments. She continued to reach out, to send messages of love and hope, believing that one day they would find their way back to her.

As Jasmine embraced her new path, she found joy in the journey itself. She set new goals, pursued further education, and found a job that aligned with her passion for animal welfare. These steps were not just about rebuilding her life but about rediscovering herself and her place in the world.

Her story was one of transformation. Jasmine learned to forgive herself for past mistakes and to let go of the guilt that had weighed heavily on her heart. She found strength in her solitude, realizing that she could overcome any obstacle that came her way.

In the quiet moments, as she sat on her porch watching the sunset, Jasmine felt a deep sense of peace. She knew that her life had been a series of trials, but she also knew that these trials had shaped her into the person she is today. A person of resilience, compassion, and unwavering hope.

Jasmine's journey is a powerful reminder that even in the face of immense pain and betrayal, there is always a path to healing and redemption. Her story is a celebration of the human spirit's capacity to endure, to find meaning amid chaos, and to embrace the beauty of the journey, no matter how difficult it may be.

As she looked towards the future, Jasmine carried with her the lessons of her past, the strength she had discovered within herself, and the unwavering belief in a brighter tomorrow. Her story is a testament to the power of love, resilience, and the unbreakable spirit of a mother who never gave up on her children or herself.

Jasmine's life, though marked by hardship, is ultimately a story of hope and transformation. She found her place in the world, a place where she could make a difference, find joy in the small things, and look forward to each new day with renewed purpose and strength. And in that journey, she discovered that she was never truly alone, for her spirit, her love, and her resilience were her constant companions.

Thank you for reading! If you enjoyed this novel, I would be incredibly grateful if you could leave a review. Your feedback helps other readers discover my work and supports me as an author.

Stay connected! Follow me on social media for updates on future books, exclusive content, and behind-the-scenes insights:

Email: NSinclair2024@hotmail.com

Other Works by N. Sinclair

Author's Page:
https://www.nsinclairwrites.com/novel

Blogs Page

https://www.nsinclairwrites.com/

Services page

https://www.nsinclairwrites.com/services

At **NSinclairWrites.com**, discover the captivating world of author **Nadia Sinclair**, where storytelling and practical financial wisdom intertwine. As a versatile novelist, N. Sinclair offers a diverse range of compelling biographies and other genres that delve deep into human experiences. Additionally, the site features insightful financial blogs, providing readers with valuable tips on money management and wealth-building strategies. Whether you're seeking gripping narratives or financial empowerment, NSinclairWrites.com offers something for every reader.

Stay tuned for more exciting projects on the horizon!

Copyright © 2024

All rights reserved.

ISBN: 979-8-9915679-3-0

www.ingramcontent.com/pod-product-compliance
Lightning Source LLC
Chambersburg PA
CBHW060818190426
43197CB00038B/2014